Managing Food Safety
the 22000 Way

Managing Food Safety the 22000 Way

David Smith, Rob Politowski
and Christina Palmer

BSi

Business
Information

First published in the UK in 2007

by
BSI
389 Chiswick High Road
London W4 4AL

Typeset in Optima and Gill Sans by Monolith
Printed in Great Britain by MPG Books, Bodmin, Cornwall

British Library Cataloguing in Publication Data
A catalogue record for this book is available from the British Library

ISBN 978 0 580 46405 8
BSI Ref: BIP 2078

Contents

Acknowledgements

The authors would like to thank those who have made contributions to this publication. In particular we would wish to note the technical contributions from Tracey Jackson-Smith of Royall International and the editing by Chris Millidge.

Additionally, Jonathan Silver of BSI has been most supportive in his constructive comments which have been much appreciated.

Foreword

The safety of the food we eat has always been of prime concern. In today's world, with the increasing level of large-scale food production and the growing levels of movement of food around the world, managing food safety has become a more challenging issue, and the consequences of any failure have become immeasurably greater. Scares such as bovine spongiform encephalopathy (BSE) and salmonella have accentuated the concerns.

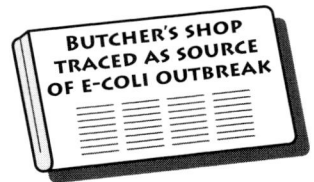

In the UK, regulations and the development of industry sector-led standards recognize the need for more formal controls and are designed to enhance food safety and therefore protect the consumer. Industry has adopted such standards as a means of protecting its reputation, satisfying its customers and consumers, and as a tool to aid compliance with food safety legislation.

The development by the International Organization for Standardization (ISO) of ISO 22000:2005, *Food safety management systems — Requirements for any organization in the food chain,* is in response to a need for greater harmonization of food safety management standards that are prevalent around the world and is designed to help organizations to comply with relevant food safety legislation as well as customer requirements in a structured and systematic way. Many organizations in the food industry will have already applied standards such as ISO 9001:2000, *Quality management systems — requirements* and will find the approach used in ISO 22000 totally consistent and compatible with such standards. Equally, those who are not

experienced in the use of formal standards will find the steps in the book easy to follow.

This book has been published for those organizations seeking to adopt ISO 22000, recognizing that this could well become the international norm in the same way that ISO 9001 has become established as the approach for quality management (now adopted by about 700,000 organizations worldwide). ISO 22000 covers the generally recognized key elements of prerequisite programmes, system management and interactive communications; integrates the principles of Hazard Analysis and Critical Control Point (HACCP) developed by the Codex Alimentarius Commission; and provides a business framework for managing food safety which is consistent with other management disciplines. This book is intended to be used in conjunction with the standard.

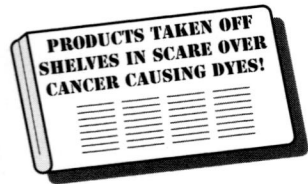

This book also recognizes that within the food industry there has traditionally been a distinction between food safety and food quality. The matter of safety is of such overriding importance that it is regarded as a separate subject in its own right, while the term 'quality' refers to all other food characteristics required to meet the demands of the consumer. ISO 22000 addresses food safety aspects only.

Guidance is additionally given for those who seek to incorporate these requirements within their overall management system using PAS 99:2006, *Specification of common management system requirements as a framework for integration* as a basis for an integrated management system. This specification has been developed to help organizations who have multiple formal management systems and wish to minimize the duplication of arrangements and procedures where there is a crossover of similar requirements. The common requirements are typically greater than 50 per cent and hence a holistic approach reduces the time needed for auditing and reviewing and helps managers adopt a more cohesive approach.

1

Introduction

The globalization of food and food products, together with the large-scale production and manufacturing processes used in the food industry, have emphasized the need for stringent control of food safety more than ever before. A food safety problem can potentially result in food-borne illnesses and in some cases death. These arise in many countries and lead to the long-term public disenchantment with those products which give rise to such problems and permanently damage the reputation of the supplier.

The public's perception of risk is such that it probably overreacts to food scares whether they are about safety or general health concerns over well-being. If organizations do not respond quickly, honestly and sensitively to public concern, then the consequences can be enormous even for large organizations. This has been recognized for a number of years and there is substantial legislation in place to protect the community from unsafe food (see Annex 2).

In considering the impact of poor food safety, it is necessary to consider the complete food chain – 'from farm to fork'. Many may have forgotten or will not be aware of the fate of Japanese fishermen at Minemata, a Japanese fishing village. In the late 1960s and early 1970s it is reputed that residents of the village noted the strange behaviour of cats climbing cliffs and jumping off. At the same time, workers in a nearby factory became ill with unusual symptoms. There were many variations in the symptoms but a doctor found mercury in the blood of one patient. This led to the discovery that mercury was being discharged from drainage pipes which then entered the food chain via simple crustaceans, then to fish and then to humans. Heavy metals can be extremely harmful to the human body.

At the other end of the food chain, the retailer or fast food outlet may provide food that is unsuitable. This might be because the food was already contaminated when procured or became so because of poor hygiene conditions at point of sale. There have been many notable cases over the last 20 years of failures in the sourcing of ingredients, food processing and at the retail end of the food chain. The results of such failures can be widespread. Apart from the human misery caused, the effect on the reputation of the supplier of the defective goods can be catastrophic and the image of the entire food industry damaged. What is more, the penalties can be very substantial, so a failure of control in food safety can result in the business failing and individuals and the organization being penalized.

According to the *Food and Drink Federation (Foodlink)*:

'Each year it is estimated that as many as 5.5 million people in the UK may suffer from foodborne illnesses – that's 1 in 10 people.'

There was a substantial increase in food poisoning in the early 1990s, but this began to slow down towards the end of the century. Since the turn of the century, there has been some reduction in food poisoning, but the statistics show that there is still much room for improvement (*Food and Drink Federation (Foodlink), 2006*). The whole food chain often has numerous links in it and these all need to be recognized and controlled to ensure that the food is safe. ISO 22000:2005 provides a framework for managing food safety and shows the links that need to be controlled. The food chain extends from farming of crops, animal feed, livestock and fish through to food producers, processing of ingredients, and food manufacture, through to wholesale, retail, food service operations and caterers to consumers, all connected by transportation and warehousing.

An example of communications and links in the food chain is shown in Figure 1.

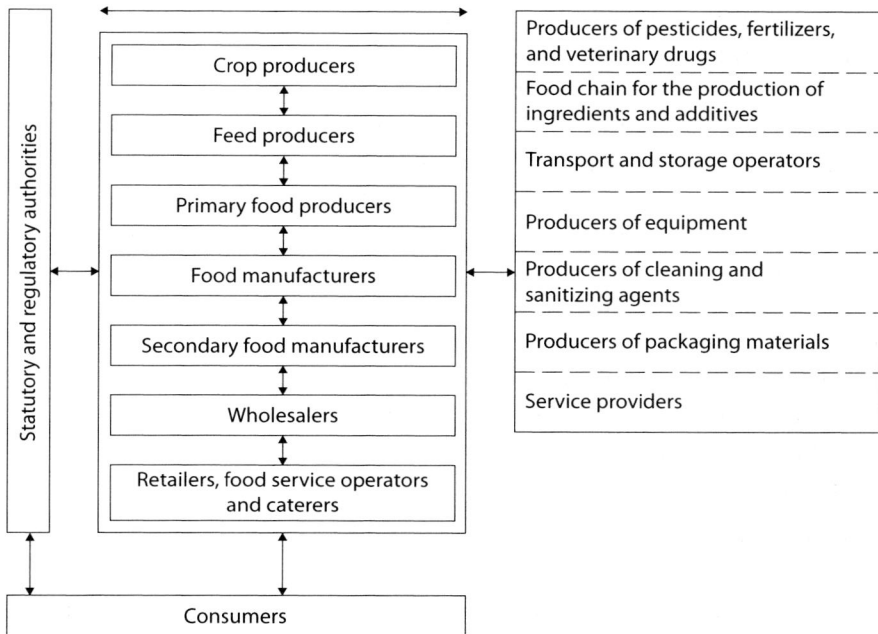

	Producers of pesticides, fertilizers, and veterinary drugs
Crop producers	
	Food chain for the production of ingredients and additives
Feed producers	
	Transport and storage operators
Primary food producers	
	Producers of equipment
Food manufacturers	
	Producers of cleaning and sanitizing agents
Secondary food manufacturers	
	Producers of packaging materials
Wholesalers	
	Service providers
Retailers, food service operators and caterers	

Consumers

Statutory and regulatory authorities

NOTE The figure does not show the type of interactive communications along and across the food chain that by-pass immediate suppliers and customers.

Source: ISO 22000:2005

Figure 1 – Example of communication within the food chain

The UK Food and Safety Act of 1990 requires all sectors to exercise reasonable precautions with respect to food sold to the public. In response to the requirement placed on retailers, the British Retail Consortium (BRC) developed the *BRC Global Standard – Food*. This has served the consumer and suppliers well in many ways. It has provided a common methodology for independent and third-party inspection used by food retailers in the UK, instead of having multiple schemes that food processors for instance may need to satisfy to meet the requirements of the different supermarket chains. In other countries and other sectors of the food industry similar types of auditing and inspection schemes have been developed, including agricultural produce, animal feed, food processing, suppliers to food retailers and fast food chains.

Internationally, there has been significant take up of the ISO 9001:2000 quality management systems specification, and there are about 700,000 organizations certified to this standard. There will be many more that have adopted this standard and have either not sought certification or are working towards it. A proportion of these will be in the food sector, whether it be farmers growing avocados and pecan nuts overseas, or manufacturers that sell to supermarkets, hotels or fast food chains. It has therefore almost been a natural progression to develop an international standard which deals with food safety in a similar and effective way to which ISO 9001 systems deliver quality. ISO 22000:2005 has been developed to fulfil such a need.

ISO 22000:2005:

– does not conflict with the schemes developed by the different sectors of the food industry, e.g. *BRC Global Standard – Food*;
– is intended to provide a management framework against which an organization can be assessed to see if it has effective controls in place to provide safe food;
– provides a management framework for identifying food hazards, determining control measures to be managed within HACCP plans, operational prerequisite programmes and managing the whole process of food safety management.

The food industry is one of the largest industries worldwide and it is appropriate that an international consensus standard has been developed to help organizations. In the fullness of time it is quite probable that the numbers associated with this standard will approach those who have adopted ISO 9001 in the food chain and it will therefore become the trade standard for food safety management systems throughout the world.

It is therefore appropriate that those organizations who already supply food products abroad should move down the road of implementing ISO 22000. Similarly, those that have ISO 9001 and are seeking to integrate their food safety management requirements into their arrangements for managing quality systems will find this approach consistent with their existing arrangements and easy to adopt. The benefits for them are the reduction in duplication, conflict, management time and effort devoted to planning, implementation, auditing, inspections and external assessment by customers or certification bodies.

Managing Food Safety the 22000 Way gives a simple approach for those wishing to take on this standard and should be used in conjunction with it. The standard contains all the requirements that are needed, but the order may give some readers difficulty should they follow the sequential approach. *Managing Food Safety the 22000 Way* gives guidance on one approach, but it is by no means the only one.

This book follows a similar approach to that adopted in *Managing Safety the Systems Way* and *Managing the Environment the 14001 Way* which have been proven to be successful. It is based on the plan, do, check, act (PDCA) approach which particularly lends itself to the HACCP methodology. HACCP is the approach required by regulation throughout Europe for those involved in the food chain.

For those organizations with systems already in place, the management framework used is the one given in PAS 99:2006, *Specification of common management system requirements as a framework for integration.* The methodology is such that those organizations seeking to implement ISO 22000:2005 systems and integrate them with other requirements from other management system specifications will find this approach helpful. This should enable integration without duplication.

To help the reader, this book includes a chapter entitled 'Getting started', which is often the most difficult stage for those with little in place (see Chapter 2). A simple methodology is offered, showing the various steps. Checklists are provided, and in addition the various steps are illustrated by examples.

A series of workbooks has been published in conjunction with this handbook that are consistent with the approach we have adopted here. They are intended to be a practical guide to members of the food safety team and managers, giving the basics of the ISO 22000 system and how to implement it. The three workbooks (BIP 2127, *ISO 22000 Food Safety: Guidance and*

Workbook for the Catering Industry; BIP 2128, *ISO 22000 Food Safety: Guidance and Workbook for the Manufacturing Sector;* and BIP 2129, *ISO 22000 Food Safety: Guidance and Workbook for the Retail Industry)* are specifically directed at those in the catering, retail and food production sectors.

2

Getting started

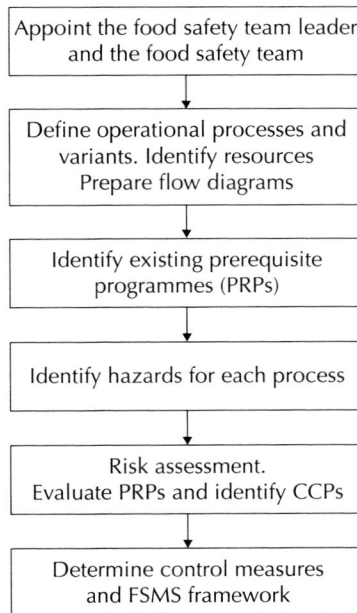

Appoint the food safety team leader
and the food safety team

Define operational processes and
variants. Identify resources
Prepare flow diagrams

Identify existing prerequisite
programmes (PRPs)

Identify hazards for each process

Risk assessment.
Evaluate PRPs and identify CCPs

Determine control measures
and FSMS framework

*Figure 2 – Steps in the implementation of a
food safety management system*

2.1 Overview

For those organizations with some sort of food safety management system in place, ISO 22000 will not be a major challenge as they will already be meeting many of the specified requirements of this standard. For those beginning with little in place, the task of implementation can be daunting and some guidance is given below on how to set up a system in such circumstances. There are basic requirements you need before even starting to set up the system and these relate to the appointment of a food safety team leader (Clause 5.5) and a food safety team (Clause 7.3.2). They are required to set up the system (Clause 4.1) and the specification for these three items needs to be addressed from the very beginning.

(Throughout this book, clause references relate to ISO 22000:2005 unless otherwise stated.)

The diagram given at the beginning of this chapter gives an indication of the stages an organization might adopt for getting started. The order is not intended to be prescriptive and some issues may be addressed in tandem with others or in a different order in some cases.

It is necessary to understand some of the fundamental terms used for the management of food safety that will be encountered in both this book and the standard itself.

> ### PRP
> ### prerequisite programme
> *<food safety> basic conditions and activities that are necessary to maintain a hygienic environment throughout the* **food chain** *(3.2) suitable for the production, handling and provision of safe* **end products** *(3.5) and safe food for human consumption…*
>
> *(Clause 3.8)*

Examples of a prerequisite programme would include maintenance schedules, cleaning schedules, design of the workplace and equipment, storage conditions, and so on.

operational PRP
operational prerequisite programme
PRP *(3.8) identified by the hazard analysis as essential in order to control the likelihood of introducing **food safety hazards** (3.3) to and/or the contamination or proliferation of food safety hazards in the product(s) or in the processing environment*

(Clause 3.9)

CCP
critical control point
*<food safety> step at which control can be applied and is essential to prevent or eliminate a **food safety hazard** (3.3) or reduce it to an acceptable level...*

(Clause 3.10)

Some of the abbreviations used are as follows:

- FSMS   food safety management system
- HACCP   hazard analysis and critical control point
- IMS   integrated management system
- ISR   initial status review
- FSTL   Food Safety Team Leader
- FS   food safety
- FSM   food safety management
- PAS   publicly available specification

Having appointed the team (see 2.2, *Appointing the team and identifying the basic needs*), there is a need to identify what is needed for the management system and what is already in place. There is also a need for sources of information on the hazards, regulatory requirements, best practice and so on, when setting up of the team is addressed; what is needed for the management system is defined in subsequent chapters.

In subsequent sections, guidance is given on the information sources that may help in setting up the system. By the end of the process, it should be possible to answer most of the questions that have to be addressed in order to set up a food safety management system (FSMS) that meets the requirements of ISO 22000.

For any organization wishing to establish a new FSMS, the first and most important step is to identify what is needed for an effective system and what arrangements and controls are already in place that might be utilized and built upon. A status review can be useful for those organizations that are unclear as to what might be needed over and above their current arrangements in order to meet the requirements of ISO 22000.

The status review provides organizations with information on the scope, adequacy and degree of implementation of an existing management system and particularly where it stands in managing food safety.

For a newly established organization, it serves to determine what arrangements are needed to ensure effective FSMS functions and the statutory and customer obligations it has to meet. The status review essentially answers the question: precisely where is the organization now in managing food safety issues and/or where does it want to be?

Carrying out the review may, at first sight, seem an onerous task. Most organizations soon find, however, that the process demonstrates that food safety is already part, if not the heart, of their existing management arrangements. It may well not be formalized and may be working in an ad hoc way because existing employees recognized the importance of specific controls. The initial status review helps organizations find out:

−   where they are currently in managing food safety issues;
−   what needs to be done to meet the organization's food safety obligations;
−   what help and information are available from internal and outside sources;
−   which of this information is relevant to the organization; and
−   how the organization shapes up to meeting the core elements of ISO 22000.

When working through this chapter, the reader should ignore those aspects that have been dealt with adequately by the existing arrangements (such as their ISO 9001 system, HACCP and/or their BRC systems) unless there is a need to benchmark.

For those readers who are new to the principles of food safety management and management systems, a case study is provided in text boxes.

Di Longcroft's Residential Conference Centre, Holbeton

Di Longcroft had spent many years in industry in a managerial capacity and had until recently spent much of her time training. She decided to retire early and set up her own international training and conference facility near to the coast in the south-west of the UK.

She had a great deal of experience in quality systems and occupational health and safety. As her centre was to provide the opportunity for some outward-bound training as part of management team-building, she decided to implement an integrated management system. Upon investigation, she discovered there was also a standard ISO 22000:2005 on food safety management and that this in theory should complement her ISO 9001 (quality management system) and OHSAS 18001 (occupational health and safety) systems she had decided to implement.

The facility was new and it was an ideal opportunity to establish what she should put in place, where there was to be the production of food products for use on outward-bound courses, as well as providing excellent menus for those attending training at the centre. She also recognized that some of her guests would be wishing to acquire snacks and she has had installed vending machines to sell sandwiches and other items that were prepared in the centre's kitchen.

She realized she had no idea where to start. Upon closer consideration of the matter, however, she developed a plan based on the model shown at the beginning of this chapter. Throughout this chapter, there are examples that apply to this establishment, as this organization (DLRCC) moves forward.

2.2 Appointing the team and identifying the basic needs

```
┌─────────────────────────┐
│   Appoint FS Team Leader │
│      and FS Team         │
└─────────────────────────┘
            │
            ▼
```

ISO 22000 identifies the requirements for the system in 4.1 General requirements, and how a team should be formed (Clause 7.3.2) under the leadership of a "food safety team leader" as specified in Clause 5.5. The wording of the requirements of the standard is explicit and therefore little additional explanation is given.

2.2.1 The food safety team leader (Clause 5.5)

The appointment of a competent food safety team leader (FSTL) is the recommended first step. This person is required to:

–   manage a food safety team and organize its work;
–   ensure relevant training and education of the food safety team members;
–   ensure that a food management system is established, implemented, maintained and updated; and
–   report to the organization's top management on the effectiveness and suitability of the food safety management system.

This appointment is crucial to the success of the operation. It may well be that the organization does not have anyone within the organization with sufficient skills to undertake this task. There may also be a significant resource issue, particularly if the appointee has other substantial duties to perform.

The FSTL will need a number of skills to meet the specified requirements. The appointee will need to be able to lead a multi-disciplined team and identify the training needs for him/herself and the members of the food safety team.

Apart from the skills previously stated and the ability to implement the system, the FSTL will need to report to the organization's top management. This can be a challenging task, as the information that he/she may be communicating may well not always be welcome and there may be a need for tact and diplomacy, so people skills and management skills, as well as knowledge of food safety, are essential skills of the FSTL. Communication needs to take into account the literacy skills of employees, e.g. those whose first language is not English, and this may require innovative approaches.

2.2.2 Appoint food safety team

The requirements for a food safety team are as follows.

> ...The food safety team shall have a combination of multi-disciplinary knowledge and experience in developing and implementing the food safety management system. This includes, but need not be limited to, the organization's products, processes, equipment and food safety hazards within the scope of the food safety management system.
> Records shall be maintained that demonstrate that the food safety team has the required knowledge and experience...

> (Clause 7.3.2)

The requirement makes it quite clear that those appointed to this role have a challenging task. The knowledge requirements about the various operational processes and about the equipment, products and the food safety-related matters highlight the need for significant competence for those appointed to the team.

It is likely that there will be some training needs for those appointed to the team, which, it is to be hoped, should complement the skills of the leader. The team needs to reflect operational knowledge of the processes used within the organization to produce the various food products. The team members need to have knowledge about the equipment, the maintenance issues and the food product and potential food safety hazards associated with them.

It is now recognized that competence of employees is one of the key issues for the effective implementation of any of the management system specifications, such as ISO 9001:2000 (quality management), ISO 14001:2004 (environmental management) and OHSAS 18001:1999 (occupational health and safety management). It is equally true for ISO 22000. The organization needs to determine what competencies are needed and then set about developing such competence within the organization or employing those with the necessary skills for this task. Competency can be achieved by training, education, knowledge and on-the-job coaching, or a mixture of these. Training should not be seen as the only necessary component, as some personnel can be trained many times and still not be competent.

Di Longcroft's Residential Conference Centre, Holbeton
A general manager had been appointed to run DLRCC, but this role was to focus on running the business as a whole. The proprietress recognized that apart from excellent chefs and kitchen staff needed to ensure that residents felt that they were privileged to stay at a 4-star plus centre there was a need to appoint someone for ensuring DLRCC met the requirements of the various training organizations that used the facilities, the quality systems and occupational health and safety arrangements. The appointment of a systems manager for quality and safety had been made but consideration had not been given to appointing someone specifically within the organization to address the implementation of an ISO 22000 system. It was decided therefore to acquire the services of someone from an agency or a consultancy as FSTL. This was not seen as a long-term solution necessarily but allowed them to move forward more quickly. A budget was provided for training the key personnel who were to form the food safety team. This included the quality and safety manager.

In-house training was provided on HACCP and ISO 22000 by an external organization within the first two months of the team being established.

The food safety team comprised the second chef, a key kitchen worker, *maître d'hôtel* and the maintenance manager. The reason for the selection was that they needed to understand the processes and the hazards associated with:

- purchasing of ingredients, equipment;
- specification of ingredients and equipment purchased;
- storage of ingredients whether frozen, chilled or ambient;
- storage of cooked or prepared food;
- maintenance of equipment;
- kitchen preparation and cooking;
- kitchen cleaning;
- serving of food; and
- filling, emptying and cleaning of vending machines.

2.2.3 Developing a food safety management system

It can be seen from the above that the appointments to food safety team is key to the success of the implementation project for ISO 22000 and its continuing effectiveness. The team is required to establish, document, implement and maintain an effective food safety management system on behalf of the organization.

The reason why this is important is that the foundation of the system is dependent upon the food safety team determining the scope and needs of the food safety management system. Should they not do a thorough job at this stage, then the foundation of the system will not be sound and problems may occur, resulting in major difficulties.

The European Community Regulation No. 852/2004 on the hygiene of foodstuffs specifies the implementation of procedures based on the HACCP principles and the food safety team will need to understand how to apply this approach and how it might be applied to the processes that the organization uses to produce its product. Such understanding can be achieved through training in the principles and application of HACCP either internally within an organization that already has this expertise or through the attendance of training with reputable training organizations.

Clause 4.1 sets out specific requirements for the development of an FSMS, namely:

- defining the scope of the food safety management system including the products, sites, processes (internal and outsourced);
- identification of food safety hazards and implementation of associated control measures;
- internal communication on the system and food safety of products;
- communication with interested parties within the food chain on food safety issues related to its products; and
- periodic evaluation of the food safety management system in order to enable updating of and improvement in the system.

These requirements give a good picture of the type of knowledge, skills and expertise required of the team leader and the members of the food safety team. The intention of having a team is to ensure that the balance of skills is there to undertake this task. It should be borne in mind that there needs to be an understanding of how the organization fits into the food chain as shown in Figure 3. More details about setting up the system are given in Chapter 3.

```
┌─────────────────────────────┐ ⎫
│        Crop producers       │ ⎬
└─────────────────────────────┘ ⎪
              ↓                   ⎪   Farmers, meat production
┌─────────────────────────────┐ ⎬   Fishermen, those producing
│        Feed producers       │ ⎪   feed for livestock
└─────────────────────────────┘ ⎪
              ↓                   ⎪
┌─────────────────────────────┐ ⎪
│    Primary food producers   │ ⎭
└─────────────────────────────┘
              ↓
┌─────────────────────────────┐ ⎫
│      Food manufacturers     │ ⎬
└─────────────────────────────┘ ⎪
              ↓                   ⎬   Manufacturing of food products
┌─────────────────────────────┐ ⎪
│  Secondary food manufacturers│ ⎭
└─────────────────────────────┘
              ↓
┌─────────────────────────────┐ ⎫
│         Wholesalers         │ ⎬
└─────────────────────────────┘ ⎪
              ↓                   ⎬   Retail, catering and wholesale
┌─────────────────────────────┐ ⎪
│ Retailers, food service     │ ⎪
│   operators and caterers    │ ⎭
└─────────────────────────────┘
```

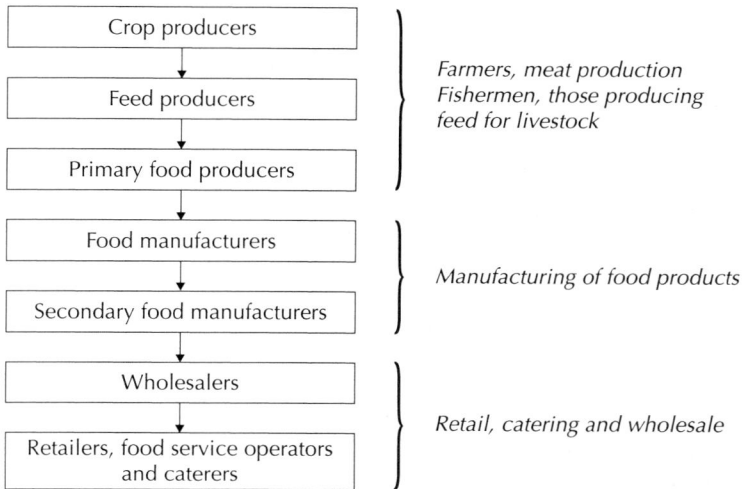

Figure 3 – The food chain

Di Longcroft's Residential Conference Centre, Holbeton
It was indeed fortunate that the systems manager had a good knowledge of management systems. He recognized that there were many common requirements specified within quality and safety management systems and that these were also common in ISO 22000. He agreed to establish a way for setting up the most efficient system that would provide for quality and safe food. First, though, there was a general recognition that they needed to identify the processes and the position in the food chain before they defined the scope of their system (requirement of Clause 4.1).

2.3 Defining operational processes

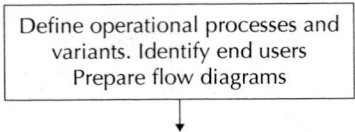

```
┌─────────────────────────────────┐
│  Define operational processes and│
│     variants. Identify end users │
│        Prepare flow diagrams     │
└─────────────────────────────────┘
                 ↓
```

As stated above, Clause 4.1 of the standard requires that the organization determine and define the scope of the system. The organization should:

– identify its main products;
– identify variants;
– consider the sites and locations from which it will operate;
– consider the internal processes; and
– consider external processes (supply, transport, delivery, and so on).

Those organizations with an ISO 9001 management system in place will already have mapped their processes. ISO 9001/4 quality management systems use the model below to show the relationship between the customer and the organization. It requires that the processes are mapped and their relationships identified.

Figure 4 shows the relationship between the customer and supplier and how the organization (the supplier) controls this product realization through management responsibility, resource management and measurement, analysis and improvement.

In the food sector the organization may have a number of customers, for example a farmer could sell produce at a farmers' market, to supermarkets and/or as feedstock to another food-producing organization. The control on the product realization stage of the various processes will need to be orientated to satisfy the particular customer. The organization therefore needs to identify its customers and their specific needs and where they fit in the food chain. The level of control may well need to be different for every customer. It should be noted that the term 'customers' is used here in the broadest sense and would include meeting regulatory and statutory requirements.

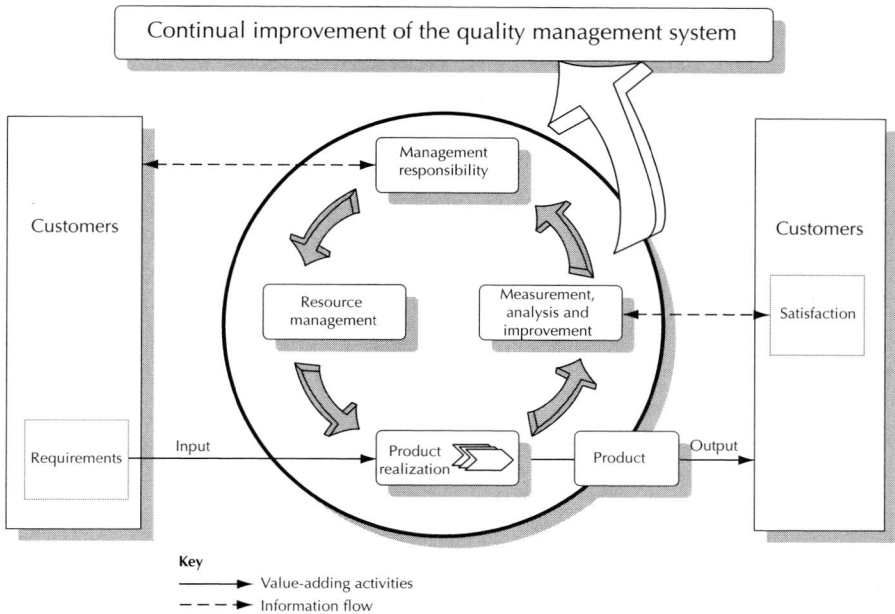

Continual improvement of the quality management system

Customers

Management responsibility

Resource management

Measurement, analysis and improvement

Customers

Satisfaction

Requirements

Input

Product realization

Product

Output

Key

→ Value-adding activities

- - -► Information flow

Source: ISO 9001:2000

Figure 4 – Quality management process model

The first stage is process mapping. It may be you are only aware in the first instance of the goods and services you buy in (inputs) and the goods and services you provide to your customers (outputs). In practice this breaks down into a number of processes.

The approach suggested here is that the processes are identified and then mapped to show their inputs and outputs. In order to do this all the inputs to your products need to be systematically identified and the output of each process determined. In simple terms the relationship between inputs and outputs can be represented as shown in Figure 5.

The output from one process, such as stored items may well form the input to another process. There will be many processes in practice and the interrelationship needs to be understood.

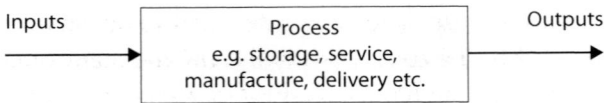

Figure 5 – Input/output relationship

This is a good framework for the organization to use for enabling it to identify the hazards that could arise.

Those with an HACCP system in place will know this process well. It is a requirement under the UK Hygiene Regulations 2006 that organizations develop procedures based on HACCP evaluation. This enables an organization to determine any part of the processes that pose a risk to food safety.

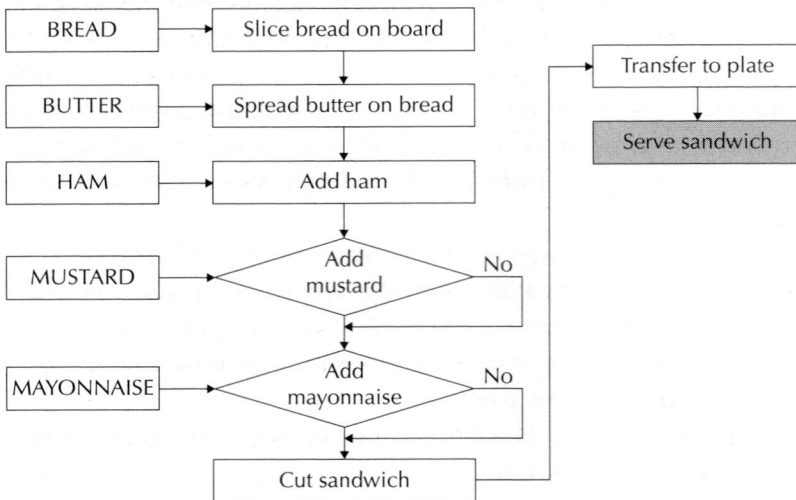

Figure 6 – Simple flow chart: Ham sandwich

Figure 6 illustrates the point that organizations need to consider the ingredient INPUTS (bread, butter, ham, mustard/mayonnaise), the preparation

PROCESS steps (slicing bread, spreading butter, and so on) and the OUTPUTS product (the sandwich!). The current law in the UK and many other countries requires that the organization has a documented system for the traceability of food products on a 'one-step-up and one-step-down' basis. This means that the food ingredient inputs must be recorded, showing details of the supplier, date, items, quantities and any batch/lot/storage details that enables the identification of their utilization. Where product outputs are supplied to other businesses there is a need to identify their details, along with any control checks made at the point of delivery. Supplies (i.e. inputs) to your business may be common to a number of different products (e.g. bread from one supplier used in many different sandwich varieties).

The above flowchart example uses a familiar process to show the principle. In practice the organization will need to look at a number of things on a broader scale. All of the processes in your business will need to be viewed in this way, and the 'inputs' and 'outputs' will extend beyond product ingredients and finished products. There is a need to consider the actual process itself to ensure the risks are controlled. If there are many types of sandwiches being made there will be a need to ensure there is no cross-contamination, say, between the ham sandwich production using ordinary bread and the bread specifically used for customers who have allergies, e.g. nuts, gluten.

For ISO 22000 compliance you will need to consider information inputs, such as the validity of any scientific data on which you base your risk assessments and controls. Outputs will also cover communication outputs, such as monitoring data used to verify and/or review the system and information for enforcement agencies.

On this basis, controls should be applied to reduce the unacceptable risks associated with the hazards.

2.4 Identify hazards, PRPs, CCPs and control measures

Di Longcroft's Residential Conference Centre, Holbeton
In very broad terms the system for DLRCC needed to cover:

Core processes

– the selection of raw materials;
– sourcing of raw materials from suppliers that could demonstrate quality and food safety;
– inspection of raw materials at delivery to the DLRCC to ensure they meet DLRCC food safety requirements;
– storage conditions (frozen, chilled, ambient) of raw materials;
– control of the actual processes involved in food production and catering (for external functions);
– appropriate segregated storage areas for the various forms of foodstuffs (e.g. recognizing the vegetarian diets and others that needed to be carefully controlled, frozen, chilled or ambient foods, cooked vs. raw foods);
– conditions for serving of food whether raw or cooked, segregated to take account of different dietary needs, allergies and time/temperature (e.g. under ambient, chilled, heated temperatures); and
– filling, emptying, cleaning the vending machines.

Supporting processes

– cleaning equipment (dishwashers, etc.);
– hygiene standards by all personnel;
– waste facilities that did not attract vermin, etc.;
– stock rotation and general housekeeping;
– pest control;
– hygiene training for all personnel;
– selection and design of facilities to aid maintenance and cleaning; and
– design of kitchen and facilities to prevent the introduction of, eliminate or minimize food safety hazards (e.g. minimize microbial problems, cross-contamination, infestation and to aid traceability).

2.4.1 Identify hazards

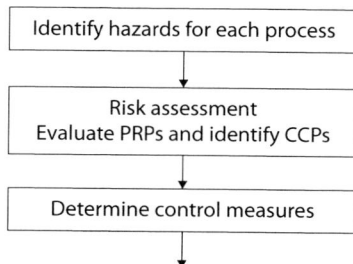

```
┌─────────────────────────────────────┐
│   Identify hazards for each process  │
└─────────────────────────────────────┘
                   │
                   ▼
┌─────────────────────────────────────┐
│          Risk assessment             │
│   Evaluate PRPs and identify CCPs    │
└─────────────────────────────────────┘
                   │
                   ▼
┌─────────────────────────────────────┐
│      Determine control measures      │
└─────────────────────────────────────┘
                   │
                   ▼
```

The UK and EU regulations require that organizations carry out HACCP-based procedures for all their processes. Those already operating in the food sector will be well aware of this requirement and how they have applied it.

In the simple case of making a ham sandwich (see Figure 6), there are very obvious areas that need control. The integrity of the ingredients supply is vital to ensure that the product is not contaminated before you even start; storage temperatures of the butter, ham and mayonnaise must be kept within legal limits to minimize the growth of harmful micro-organisms; and the process activities should indicate steps at which potential cross-contamination needs to be controlled. The first stage of the hazard analysis is to identify all of these potential hazards that could harm your customer, and your business, and then to evaluate the risk that they each pose.

Identifying these hazards requires some food safety expertise, particularly in relation to microbiological contamination and growth. Information regarding pathogen risks for specific food types, along with their growth factors such as A_w, pH and temperature range is necessary for the accurate and complete identification of potential hazards and will inform subsequent decisions as to appropriate controls. Reference to valid, externally published scientific and technical data is vital for an effective HACCP plan and operational PRP and this can be accessed through a variety of industry sources.

There are a number of areas where the organization should examine its current FSMS arrangements when undertaking an initial status review to judge what is required where no formal management system exists, or if the organization is newly established.

The following lists a few areas for consideration:

1. Fundamental to every successful FSMS is the implementation of prerequisite programmes (PRPs) and HACCP plans – across normal, abnormal and potential emergency operational conditions. The organization needs to establish what current PRP and HACCP plans exist. The current arrangements need to be reviewed to establish whether they are adequate.
2. All companies have to be compliant with some specific statutory provisions that govern food safety – these regulations need to be identified and assessed. The current arrangements need to be reviewed to establish whether they are adequate.
3. The customer's requirements need to be identified and understood and arrangements implemented to deliver these requirements – the current arrangements need to be reviewed to establish whether they are adequate.
4. Very few organizations are so unique that they have no peers. Consequently, areas of best operational food safety practice should be identified and reviewed for suitability and potential adoption.
5. Although organizations can be similar in their management delivery, they are rarely the same and, as such, all guidance and best practice taken for the organization will need to be tailored to its particular needs before it is implemented. Implementation can only be achieved when it is communicated and briefed to those who need it. The current arrangements for internal communications need to be reviewed.
6. Often what employees perceive as the 'only solution' is successfully adapted by them to work in a more effective way. Sometimes such adaptations can be problematic but in many cases it may be worthwhile adopting the 'established' practice if it meets the organization's needs.
7. The initial status review will determine how best to measure FSMS effectiveness. Many areas will respond to conventional audit and inspection techniques – these will be identified together with the need for more specialist tools (e.g. product testing). The current arrangements need to be reviewed to establish whether they are adequate.

8. As with all aspects of business performance, review processes should exist to monitor management system effectiveness and identify what subsequent objectives are established to enable continual improvement and updating of the FSMS. The current arrangements need to be reviewed to establish whether they are adequate.

Checklist 1 is provided to assist when identifying hazards. Mark "Yes" if applicable, and "No" if not.

CHECKLIST 1 – Identifying hazards

Biological (e.g bacteria, such as salmonella, e-coli, campylobacter)

Yes No
☐ ☐ Food-poisoning bacteria
☐ ☐ Viruses
☐ ☐ Microscopic parasites

Sources of the above can be:
- Raw food   • People
- Pets and pests   • Air and dust
- Water   • Soil
- Food waste

Physical hazards (e.g. plastic, glass, wood, metal, insects, paper)
☐ ☐ Stones, pips, leaves or stalks from fruit and vegetables
☐ ☐ Shell fragments from nuts, shellfish and eggs
☐ ☐ Scales from fish, bone fragments from poultry and meat, feathers
☐ ☐ Paper, string, plastic or staples from food packaging
☐ ☐ Nuts, bolts and screws from machinery or equipment
☐ ☐ Fragments of glass or china
☐ ☐ Jewellery, hair, fingernails, buttons, pen tops and plasters
☐ ☐ Dust and dirt from the air, rubbish or unclean equipment
☐ ☐ Insects, their eggs and droppings

Chemical (e.g. pesticide and fertilizer residues, cleaning agents)
☐ ☐ Cleaning chemicals
☐ ☐ Industrial processing chemicals, oils and greases
☐ ☐ Agricultural chemicals
☐ ☐ Pesticides and pest bait

Di Longcroft's Residential Conference Centre, Holbeton

Following their initial training the Food Safety Team at DLRCC decided to identify hazards. It soon became clear that there were quite a number and that a structured approach to identification and planning a suitable way in which to deal with these was necessary. It was particularly important for the new centre, as it needed to demonstrate the highest standards and attention to detail if it was to make real impact in what is a highly competitive market.

DLRCC decided to review its core processes and to represent them using a flow diagram which identified each step in their process from receipt of ingredients through to serving of food and stocking vending machines. Once they had done this, they then conducted an investigation into each step to identify the potential food safety hazards, categorize them and describe the reason for the potential presence of each hazard.

2.4.2 Primary legislation and regulation

The second element of the initial status review relates to the regulatory control obligations placed on the organization, and includes the following:

- core legislation and regulations applicable to all organizational activities; and
- more specific legal responsibility which may or may not apply, either continually or as a result of the organization's activities.

There are many specific regulations and requirements that are defined within various sources that are publicly available. The list changes continually and useful weblinks for accessing this information are provided in Annex 3.

As the second part of the initial status review, the following checklist details some of the more recent and general legislation currently in force and which is applicable to many organizations. This list is by no means exhaustive and is subject to change and amendments.

Checklist 2 has been provided for you to identify general legislation and regulations that: apply to your organization (1); have been addressed (2); are not relevant (3). You may need to extend the checklist to include all other relevant legislation as part of your review.

CHECKLIST 2 – General legislation and regulations applying to the food industry in the UK

1	2	3	
☐	☐	☐	Regulation (EC) No 852/2004 on the hygiene of foodstuffs (effective 1 January 2006)
☐	☐	☐	Regulation (EC) No 853/2004 laying down specific hygiene rules for food of animal origin (effective 1 January 2006)
☐	☐	☐	Regulation (EC) No 854/2004 laying down specific rules for the organization of official controls on products of animal origin intended for human consumption (effective 1 January 2006)
☐	☐	☐	Regulation (EC) No 178/2002 on general principles and requirements of the European Food Safety Authority and laying down procedures in matters of food safety (February 2002)
☐	☐	☐	Regulation (EC) No 2073/2005 on microbiological criteria for foodstuffs (effective 1 January 2006)
☐	☐	☐	Food Hygiene (England) Regulations 2006
☐	☐	☐	Food Hygiene (Scotland) Regulations 2006
☐	☐	☐	Food Hygiene (Wales) Regulations 2006
☐	☐	☐	Food Hygiene (Northern Ireland) Regulations 2006
☐	☐	☐	Food Safety Act 1990
☐	☐	☐	Food Labelling Regulations 1996
☐	☐	☐	EU Directive No. 2000/13/EC

For further information on the legislation in Checklist 2, and other more detailed legislation and guidance, the reader may wish to consult the FSA website at http://www.food.gov.uk/ which also provides a wide range of sources of information and guidance aimed at the food industry including small businesses, farmers, growers and producers, processors, caterers, restaurants, retailers. Annex 3 provides more detailed information to help the reader.

Di Longcroft's Residential Conference Centre, Holbeton

- DLRCC reviewed the list of regulations, as well as the list of sources of information and decided that in order to determine how they would go about implementing applicable regulations to ensure that they were compliant, they would first have to get a better understanding of what food regulation applied to them and how food regulation was enforced.
- To do this the food safety team leader (FSTL) started with exploring the role of the Food Standards Agency by reviewing the content on the agency's website (http://www.food.gov.uk/).
- The FSTL found that there was a section on hygiene legislation which contained information on the new food hygiene legislation that was introduced in the UK in January 2006 and a number of associated resources. The FSTL noted that EU hygiene regulations had been incorporated into the UK food hygiene legislation. After reading through the section, the FSTL concluded that the next step to understanding what legislation was applicable would be to contact their local authority and speak to the environmental health service who is responsible for enforcement of the food hygiene regulations.
- The FSTL also noted that an HACCP system, and training of staff in food hygiene had been included as legal requirements and could see from having read ISO 22000 how implementing the standard could help with compliance with the legislation.

2.4.3 Existing information, resources, guidance and instructions within the organization

The next step involves looking at the information, guidance and instruction on food safety that you already have in place in the organization.

There will almost certainly be something in place in every organization. From the outset, all organizations have to establish at least some ground rules for food safety control. Very few operations in the food sector are conceived without some regard for food safety criteria.

Documentation covering food safety can be found in a number of the forms including:

–   guidance summarizing regulatory requirements that apply to the organization;
–   specific instructions covering the process.

It is not sufficient for an organization to say that it complies with guidance and legislation without it providing evidence of direct implementation into the organization.

Checklist 3 shows some of the safety aspects applying to organizations that should be covered by documented procedures. This checklist is not exhaustive and tickboxes are provided for you to identify those you have in place or are introducing (1), may apply (2) or are irrelevant (3).

CHECKLIST 3 – Existing food safety information, resources, guidance and instructions within the organization

1	2	3	
❑	❑	❑	Regulatory requirements that apply to the organization's activities (e.g premises, products, packaging, equipment, training, personal hygiene, water supply)
❑	❑	❑	Communication with local enforcement agency
❑	❑	❑	Communication with customers
❑	❑	❑	Top management commitment
❑	❑	❑	HACCP plans and procedures for developing them
❑	❑	❑	Prerequisite programmes and procedures for developing them

1	2	3	
☐	☐	☐	Relevant industry codes of practice and guidance
☐	☐	☐	Procedures for updating the food safety management system
☐	☐	☐	Product specifications
☐	☐	☐	Food Safety Policy
☐	☐	☐	Audits of system, HACCP, PRPs (quality, safety, etc.)
☐	☐	☐	Previous management reviews
☐	☐	☐	Food safety team leader
☐	☐	☐	Food safety team
☐	☐	☐	Emergency preparedness plans
☐	☐	☐	Procedures for selection of suppliers
☐	☐	☐	Training programme on food safety
☐	☐	☐	Product testing
☐	☐	☐	Monitoring and measurement of control measures

2.4.4 Best practice and guidance in particular industry sectors

This section covers guidance and instruction on food safety available from organizations and trade associations operating and/or specializing in similar fields of activity. Very few processes and activities found in organizations are so new that there is no existing information available about them.

Information is readily available from many easily accessible sources, ranging from suppliers who have a legal responsibility to produce guidance on the use of their products, to the FSA, Defra, trade associations and other food industry organizations.

Trade associations or similar bodies exist to support and coordinate technical developments within specific business sectors. Many produce advice and guidance focused towards their particular sector. This information is especially valuable as it is invariably based on the real-life experience of other member organizations. Frequently, regulatory bodies such as the FSA endorse this type of guidance.

Similar information can arise out of a consensus between several different operators seeking to set standards within a particular sphere of activity.

Checklist 4 shows possible sources of outside information. Tickboxes are provided for you to identify those that are relevant (1), may apply (2) or are irrelevant (3).

CHECKLIST 4 – Sources of information for your organization

1	2	3	
❏	❏	❏	Food Standards Agencies for Scotland, England, Wales
❏	❏	❏	Codex Alimentarius Commission
❏	❏	❏	Defra
❏	❏	❏	European Commission
❏	❏	❏	Publications on food hygiene and food safety
❏	❏	❏	Electronic software packages on food hygiene and food safety
❏	❏	❏	Small businesses (e.g. Small Business Service), Business Links
❏	❏	❏	Food industry trade associations and organizations (e.g. British Retail Consortium, Food and Drink Federation, British Hospitality Association, National Farmers Union, Nationwide Caterers Association, Campden and Chorleywood Food Research Association)
❏	❏	❏	Environmental health officer
❏	❏	❏	Trading standards officer
❏	❏	❏	Suppliers (e.g. product, equipment, packaging, services)
❏	❏	❏	Customers
❏	❏	❏	Business groups (e.g. Business Links, CBI)
❏	❏	❏	Standards-making bodies (e.g. ISO, CEN, BSI)

Di Longcroft's Residential Conference Centre, Holbeton

It was indeed fortunate that there was a lot of information available that gave excellent advice on what to do to meet the requirements of food safety in their sector.

The Food Standards Agency for instance provides a range of food safety and hygiene publications, such as:

–   *Food Hygiene: a Guide to Businesses*
–   *Safer Food, Better Business for Caterers*

- *Safer Food, Better Business for Retailers*
- *Eggs: What Caterers Need to Know*

In addition, further information and guidance was obtained from:

- British Hospitality Association
- Business Link
- The local environmental health officer.

2.4.5 Determine what controls are needed

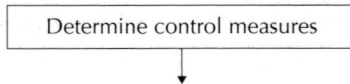

Determine control measures

The next logical step is to install controls to eliminate or significantly reduce the risk of the food product becoming unsafe.

In practice the organization may well need to look at a number of things:

- the regulatory requirements are such that organizations have to carry out HACCP assessments for all their processes. Those already operating in the food sector will be well aware of this requirement and how they have applied it;
- the regulatory requirements for their products, processes or activities;
- information on PRPs for specific products or processes;
- customer requirements for specific products and processes;
- their own experience and expertise today.

In the simple example of making a ham sandwich, there are very obvious areas that need control, e.g. storage of ingredients and stock rotation to minimize microbial growth, personal hygiene, cleaning and pest control.

2.5 Meeting the framework needs for the management system

The general requirements for a food safety management system are:

> *The organization shall establish, document, implement and maintain an effective food safety management system and update it when necessary in accordance with the requirements of this International Standard...*

(Clause 4.1)

The process of establishing, implementing and maintaining a food safety management system fits neatly into the 'plan, do, check, act' model and can be used as a quick starting point to identify which key requirements of ISO 22000 are already covered and which key requirements have yet to be established, implemented and maintained.

As stated in the introduction, PAS 99:2006, *Specification of common management system requirements as a framework for integration* is used here as a basis for implementing and operating. This model is devised so that it will enable organizations to embrace the common requirements of those specifications to which it subscribes in an integrated manner. One of the useful tools in the initial status review process is to evaluate the organization's current management system arrangements against such a formal model in order to identify any shortfalls.

In order to assess whether your organization is meeting the objectives for these model elements, Checklist 5 has been provided. A blank column has been provided for you to identify where your existing arrangements meet the needs of ISO 22000:2005 and where there are shortfalls.

CHECKLIST 5 – Objectives for model elements

Management system element	Yes	No
4.1 General requirements	❏	❏
4.2 Management system policy	❏	❏
4.3 Planning 4.3.1 HACCP and identification of control points 4.3.2 Identification of legal and other requirements 4.3.3 Contingency 4.3.4 Objectives 4.3.5 Organizational structure, roles, responsibilities and authorities	❏ ❏ ❏ ❏ ❏	❏ ❏ ❏ ❏ ❏
4.4 Implementation and operation 4.4.1 Operational control 4.4.2 Management of resources 4.4.3 Documentation requirements 4.4.4 Communication	❏ ❏ ❏ ❏	❏ ❏ ❏ ❏

4.5 Performance assessment		
4.5.1 Monitoring and measurement	❑	❑
4.5.2 Evaluation of compliance	❑	❑
4.5.3 Internal audit	❑	❑
4.5.4 Handling of nonconformities	❑	❑
4.6 Improvement		
4.6.1 General	❑	❑
4.6.2 Corrective, preventative and improvement action	❑	❑
4.7 Management review	❑	❑

In addition to the above the organization may wish to assess its current status with respect to the self-assessment questionnaire in Annex 1. This can be used as a reference point for the organization in order to determine its progress in achieving its objective of implementing an effective ISO 22000:2005 food safety management system. The above is a framework that is aligned with PAS 99. This framework makes it easier to take on board similar requirements from ISO 9001 and other specifications. The actual correspondence between PAS 99 and ISO 22000 is illustrated in Table 4 in Chapter 14.

Di Longcroft's Residential Conference Centre, Holbeton
The systems manager found that a new specification PAS 99 (see Chapter 14) had been produced which would serve his purpose for developing an integrated management system. It identified the core requirements that he needed to address for safety and general quality management and could also incorporate many of the elements needed for the food safety and quality management systems. This would allow them to take on board many of those areas where duplication would have been unnecessarily burdensome such as:

- training records;
- audit protocols and procedures;

- management reviews;
- documentation and record requirements;
- organizational structures, etc.

There were obviously specific needs for ISO 22000 and food safety management but equally there were, in particular, requirements for health and safety that had to be addressed.

The PAS 99 framework was a useful approach to assess what was in place.

3

Outline of the requirements of an FSMS

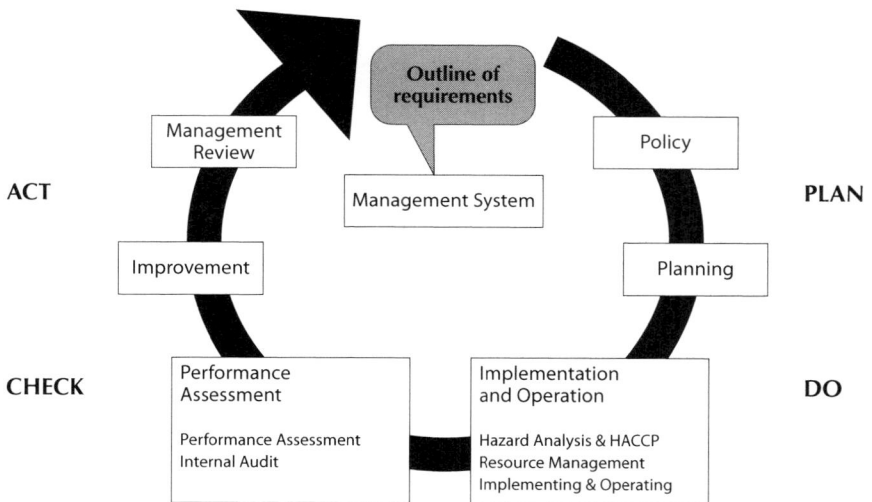

Figure 7 – Outline requirements

This chapter deals with the following clauses from ISO 22000:2005:

- General requirements   4.1
- Food safety team leader   5.5
- Food safety team   7.3.2

The foundation of the management system is specified in Clause 4.1 of ISO 22000:2005 which defines the arrangements for managing the various elements required to deliver effective food safety management. It requires:

> *The organization shall establish, document, implement and maintain an effective food safety management system and update it when necessary in accordance with the requirements of this International Standard.*
>
> *The organization shall define the scope of the food safety management system. The scope shall specify the products or product categories, processes and production sites that are addressed by the food safety management system.*
>
> *The organization shall*
>
> a) *ensure that food safety hazards that may be reasonably expected to occur in relation to products within the scope of the system are identified, evaluated and controlled in such a manner that the products of the organization do not, directly or indirectly, harm the consumer,*
>
> b) *communicate appropriate information throughout the food chain regarding safety issues related to its products,*
>
> c) *communicate information concerning development, implementation and updating of the food safety management system throughout the organization, to the extent necessary to ensure the food safety required by this International Standard, and*
>
> d) *evaluate periodically, and update when necessary, the food safety management system to ensure that the system reflects*

*the organization's activities and incorporates the most recent
information on the food safety hazards subject to control.*

*Where an organization chooses to outsource any process that
may affect end product conformity, the organization shall ensure
control over such processes. Control of such outsourced processes
shall be identified and documented within the food safety
management system.*

(Clause 4.1)

In order to achieve these objectives, an FSTL needs to be appointed
(Clause 5.5) to lead a food safety team as required by Clause 7.3.2.

The ISO 22000 food safety management system follows the 'plan, do,
check, act' model, which is the approach used in ISO 9001, 14001 and
OHSAS 18001. This entails:

– determining the scope of the system;
– system planning;
– determining relevant food safety hazards and the control measures to
  manage them within the scope of the system;
– implementation, monitoring; and
– verification and review of effectiveness of control measures and system
  to enable improvement.

3.1 Determining the scope of the system

The scope should be appropriate to the nature and scale of the organization's
activities, products and processes. Outsourced activities and processes that
impact on the food safety of the product should be included within the
scope of the system.

Consideration should be given to where the organization sits in the
food chain, and the impact this has on enabling it to manage effectively its

legal obligations, its suppliers, its food safety system and meeting customer requirements in relation to food safety and its food safety management system.

3.2 System planning

In order to start the planning phase of the system, the resources required should be identified, taking into account the level of expertise and resources available within the organization and any need to use outside expertise to help to develop an effective system. In addition a general understanding of how the organization does things as well as the generally used communication channels is important so that whoever is developing the system can do so bearing in mind the users of the system and their needs.

In practice a combination of resources internal and external to the organization may be used, but in any case an FSTL should be appointed who will manage the development, implementation and maintenance of the system and who will report to top management on progress. Depending on the resources and expertise available, the FSTL will be working with a food safety team drawn from a range of disciplines including people who understand PRPs, HACCP principles and their application, the processes and products to be included in the scope, food safety hazards (physical, chemical, microbiological) and suitable control measures.

The system planning process will involve:

- identifying the requirements for the system – what needs to be done;
- setting clear performance criteria – what is to be done;
- allocating responsibility – who gets it done;
- setting time-scales – when is it to be done by; and
- identifying the desired outcome – what the result should be.

3.3 Determining relevant food safety hazards

Food safety hazards should be identified based on the scope of the system determined and should be included within the planning phase.

Before conducting a food safety hazard analysis, the FSTL and food safety team will have been appointed.

In preparation for the hazard analysis, food safety information that should be gathered and maintained includes:

- legal obligations;
- suppliers and outsourced processes and products;
- customer requirements;
- current PRPs and/or HACCP plans in use and the need for updating and improving in light of new legal obligations, suppliers, customer requirements, recognized industry codes and standards;
- verified flow diagrams for the processes and products covered by the scope of the system, product characteristics, intended use of products and the need for improving and updating in light of new legal obligations, customer requirements;
- traceability system currently in use and the need for updating and improvement; and
- emergency procedures in place and the need for updating and improvement.

This exercise may also be covered under the initial status review of the management system.

Once the preliminary information has been collected, then the hazard analysis can be conducted. This involves:

- identification of food safety hazards in relation to the type of product, process, actual processing facilities;
- evaluation of each food safety hazard:
  — according to the possible severity of adverse health effects and likelihood of occurrence; and whether
  — the elimination or reduction of the hazard to acceptable levels is required in order to produce safe food;
- selection of appropriate control measures to be managed for each food safety hazard and whether the control measures should be managed within the operational PRPs and/or the HACCP plan;

- developing the operational PRPs;
- developing the HACCP plan;
- validation that the control measures to be used will be effective when implemented; and
- development of the plan for verifying that the control measures are effective.

3.4 Implementation and monitoring

Implementation and monitoring of operational PRPs and HACCP plans will require all those involved to understand what their role and responsibility is in implementing and monitoring an effective food safety management system. This will require giving staff the appropriate tools to carry out their jobs effectively, including communication and training programmes to be put in place for all staff and carried out at a level appropriate for the job being undertaken and the culture of the organization, including:

- the food safety hazards associated with their role;
- personal hygiene policies;
- what the controls are and how they are to be monitored and measured;
- what to do (corrective actions) when controls go outside set control limits;
- who has the authority to take decisions on nonconforming or potentially unsafe product;
- who is to be communicated with internally and externally of the organization;
- when, how and on what aspect of food safety is external communication to be conducted, e.g. customers and who in the organization is responsible for and has the authority for this activity;
- top management commitment and responsibility; and
- the food safety team role, responsibility and authority, and their roles and responsibilities in helping the organization to meet its food safety policy and objectives.

3.5 Verification and review

In order to determine whether the food safety management system is effective, the system should be verified at planned intervals. The verification plan should include the purpose, methods, frequency and responsibilities for verification. Verification can be in the form of internal, supplier, outsourced processes and/ or external audits as well as raw material, intermediate product, final product testing, and testing to verify effectiveness of, for example, cleaning systems.

Where product testing is involved, consideration should be given to the competency of the staff conducting the testing, test analysis and the test methods used.

For internal and external audits, the auditors should be competent to conduct audits. Competency will normally include both a technical under-standing of the area to be audited as well as competency in auditing skills.

Verification should be conducted to confirm that the PRPs, operational PRPs and HACCP plans are implemented, that hazards are within acceptable levels, and that any other related procedures have been implemented and are effective.

Where verification is based on testing end product samples, any samples indicating nonconforming product should be handled as potentially unsafe.

The food safety team should then undertake an analysis of the results of verification activities (internal audits, external audits, testing) and report their findings to top management for review and agree actions for improving and updating the management system.

Di Longcroft's Residential Conference Centre, Holbeton
The DLRCC implementation team found the model they had chosen based on PAS 99 particularly useful as they were able to draw on the common requirements for auditing, reviewing, etc. already developed for quality and safety systems rather than develop new processes for their ISO 22000 system.

4

Defining a food safety policy

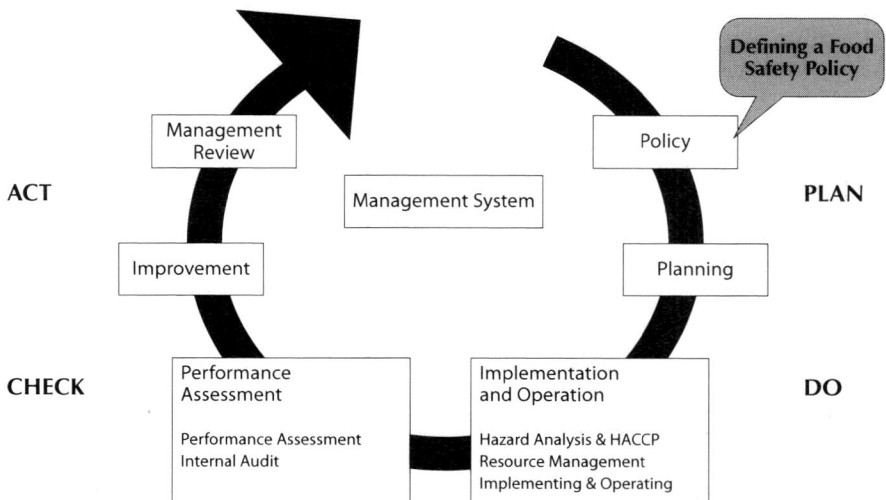

Figure 8 – Defining a food safety policy

This chapter deals with the following clauses from ISO 22000:2005:

- Management commitment   5.1
- Food safety policy   5.2

It is self-evident that an organization needs to demonstrate its commitment to managing any discipline if it is to have any credibility. Food safety management is no different in this respect. The policy is a manifestation of this commitment, providing a framework against which the organization can be evaluated. Most would agree that the requirements of ISO 22000 are not unreasonable. It considers policy issues in two parts: management commitment and food safety policy. Overall the generic requirements are very similar to those found in other management system standards. This means alignment or integration of this policy with, say, a quality system or within a PAS 99 framework should be easy to achieve.

4.1 Management commitment

ISO 22000, Clause 5.1 states:

> *Top management shall provide evidence of its commitment to the development and implementation of the food safety management system and to continually improving its effectiveness by*
>
> a) *showing food safety is supported by the business objectives of the organization,*
> b) *communicating to the organization the importance of meeting the requirements of this International Standard, any statutory and regulatory requirements, as well as customer requirements relating to food safety,*
> c) *establishing the food safety policy,*
> d) *conducting management reviews, and*
> e) *ensuring the availability of resources.*
>
> *(Clause 5.1)*

Society's expectations are increasing the pressure on organizations to reduce the risk of unsafe food, particularly as the number of reported major food scares grows, receiving greater publicity. Organizations need to achieve not only a high level of performance in their processes, but also continual

---

improvement in that performance. In addition to meeting any legal requirements, the aim should be to move forward, in a cost-effective manner, to improve food safety performance and to evolve continuously the management system to meet changing business and legislative needs. For example, it should include the 'lessons learned' from incidents, audit findings and best practice.

Unless the policy is embraced within the business objectives of the organization, it is unlikely to be effectively delivered as the necessary commitment is probably absent. The elements covering management review, availability of resources and communication are covered in separate clauses in the standard itself, and the requirements here are a manifestation that the organization is committed to deliver the processes put forward by the policy statement.

4.2 Food safety policy

In addition to Clause 5.1, there is a specific Clause (5.2) that addresses the policy requirements:

> *Top management shall define, document and communicate its food safety policy.*
> *Top management shall ensure that the food safety policy*
>
> a)   *is appropriate to the role of the organization in the food chain,*
> b)   *conforms with both statutory and regulatory requirements and with mutually agreed food safety requirements of customers,*
> c)   *is communicated, implemented and maintained at all levels of the organization,*
> d)   *is reviewed for continued suitability (see 5.8),*
> e)   *adequately addresses communication (see 5.6), and*
> f)   *is supported by measurable objectives.*
>
> *(Clause 5.2)*

It can be seen from the above that these requirements take on board what is required in Clause 5.1 (management commitment). The policy will need to be signed and dated to demonstrate this commitment by top management. Those seeking certification will be challenged at top management level to establish that they are committed to the policy and understand what is expected from the management system. Each requirement of the policy clause is dealt with in turn below with an explanation of what is expected.

4.2.1 Appropriate to the role of the organization in the food chain

The policy should be appropriate to the nature and scale of the organization's risks, recognizing the impact it could have within the food chain. The impacts should not be overstated nor trivialized but indicate that the organization has taken account of its role and its commitment to meet expectations.

4.2.2 Conformity with both statutory and regulatory requirements and with mutually agreed food safety requirements of customers

The policy should include a commitment to at least comply with currently applicable food safety legislation. It needs to comply with any specific customer requirements about its sourcing of materials, packaging, etc. If it subscribes to any voluntary programmes, codes of practice, corporate or group policies, internal standards and specifications these will need to be incorporated as well.

4.2.3 Communicated, implemented and maintained at all levels of the organization

The policy should be communicated to all employees with the intent to make them aware of their individual obligations. The involvement and participation of employees and their representatives is vital in order to gain commitment and to ensure the success of a food safety management system. Involving employees is often neglected. In most, if not all organizations, employees wish to contribute positively to the continuing success of their organization as it is their livelihood. It therefore follows that a partnership with them can be beneficial.

It is a common misconception that the only employees needing training are those directly working in operational activities. This is not the case: management at all levels should understand their responsibilities and be competent to undertake the tasks they are required to perform including managing food safety.

4.2.4 Reviewed for continued suitability

The policy should be reviewed periodically to ensure that it remains relevant and appropriate to the organization.

Change is inevitable and, as a driver of continual improvement, top management should ensure that the food safety policy is reviewed regularly in order to meet changing circumstances, such as new business demands, legislation and technology, as well as, most importantly, the lessons learned from incident investigation, audit findings and best practice.

4.2.5 Adequately addresses communication

Employees at all levels should receive appropriate communication and training to ensure that they are competent to carry out their duties and responsibilities. Training must be appropriate to the needs of each employee and to the positive benefit of the organization.

The method of communication should meet the needs of the workforce in that it should reflect their literacy and language skills. There is little value in giving them long-winded statements or instructions in complex English if this is not their main language.

4.2.6 Supported by measurable objectives

There is a need to ensure that the policy enables the identification of objectives which are measurable and which lend themselves to be audited within the organization. A policy that does not define its commitment in this manner has little meaning, as it is difficult to demonstrate that the organization is striving to achieve any improvements.

In addition to those items listed above there is a need to include those issues it commits to as identified in Clause 5.1, and so a statement on commitment to continual improvement should be included. There should be a recognition that food safety is embraced within the business and the policy should be communicated to interested parties. Checklist 6 is provided as an example of how to check your organization's policy.

CHECKLIST 6 – The policy statement of your organization

Yes	No	
❏	❏	Do you set and publish measurable and supporting objectives?
❏	❏	Is the policy appropriate to the role of the organization in the food chain?
❏	❏	Do you provide adequate and appropriate resources to implement your policy, including access to competent personnel to deliver the food safety policy?
❏	❏	Is food safety recognized and implemented as an integral part of your business performance?
❏	❏	Do you include commitment to continual cost-effective improvement in your performance?
❏	❏	Do you make management of food safety a prime responsibility of your line managers, from your most senior executive down to your first-line supervisors?
❏	❏	Do you include a commitment to comply with currently applicable legislation, and with customer and other requirements to which the organization subscribes?
❏	❏	Does the policy acknowledge that people are a key resource?
❏	❏	Do you ensure and encourage employee involvement, participation and consultation?
❏	❏	Do you allow and encourage employee involvement through all aspects of development and implementation of FS policy?
❏	❏	Are you committed to continual employee training to a level where they are able to carry out their duties competently?
❏	❏	Do you communicate your policy to all employees and ensure that they are made aware of their individual obligations?
❏	❏	Is the policy and performance made readily available to other interested parties?
❏	❏	Is your policy and management system reviewed periodically to ensure that it remains relevant and appropriate to the organization in the drive for continual improvement?

Figures 9 and 10 illustrate two example policies. These examples are provided for you to review and identify where they comply with the requirements of ISO 22000:2005.

MESS

MESS has six stores in the Midlands that specialize in providing shopping facilities. These are in modern housing estates where the residents are typically young hard-working professionals that have little time for shopping or cooking. MESS provides all their needs with respect to household goods, newspapers and prepared foods, ready meals and snacks.

Humble Meat Pies

Humble Meat Pies is a producer of high-quality meat pies. Its products are widely sold to a range of retailers across a wide geographical area. It has to deal with the complexities of the procurements of a huge variety of materials for the manufacture of meat pies.

Middle Estate Super Shops (MESS)
Food safety policy

MESS is an organization operating retail stores in the Midlands, providing household goods, prepared foods, ready meals and snacks.

At MESS we recognize our responsibility and vulnerability and that any incidence of food safety problems would have an immediate effect on our reputation. We therefore strive to maintain the highest standard in the quality and safety of our food merchandise. All the staff are comprehensively trained in food hygiene and encouraged to bring any problems to the immediate attention of managers. The managers are active in monitoring the way goods are delivered, stored and displayed and ensure that goods are arranged so that they are always within date range.

Our cooked meats, dairy produce, fish, vegetables and fruit are of the highest standard. We ensure that they are stored and displayed in the appropriate environment and temperature and we never knowingly sell old stock.

The management takes an active role in ensuring the facilities are to the highest standard and are kept clean and tidy. We provide the staff with excellent welfare facilities to enable them to maintain scrupulous hygiene standards throughout the shop and in the warehouses.

Our HACCP system is in operation and the arrangements in place meet legal requirements. We aim to improve standards on a year-by-year basis by reviewing how well our system is working and by selecting new objectives for improvement. To help us to improve we encourage ideas for improvement from our staff and customers.

Our policy is available for all to see and copies can be obtained freely from the reception by relevant interested parties.

Signed Fred Bear MD

Dated 20 Oct 2006

Figure 9 – Sample food safety policy for Middle Estate Super Shops

Humble Meat Pies
Food safety policy statement

Humble pies are the best meat pies available to man, made from the best meat cuts and covered with our unique flaky pastry. Our award-winning pies use sources of meat that are of the highest quality from selected farms where there is no compromise over quality and safety and where the animals roam freely and eat only natural food.

Humble Meat Pies will never compromise on quality and food safety, and to this end we

- inspect suppliers of all their raw materials
- ensure all storage facilities meet the highest standards
- train all staff on food hygiene and give regular refresher training
- train all managers on certified food hygiene courses to the highest level
- ensure all senior managers commit to the standards
- regularly review all the arrangements
- seek input from staff on our failings and opportunities for improvement
- monitor, inspect, verify and validate all our activities
- audit against the requirements of ISO 22000 at least every 6 months
- welcome customer comments and feedback
- ensure that those who sell our pies aspire to the same standards as us

The senior management commit to review this policy annually and the management arrangements to ensure their continuing suitability for delivering high-quality and safe meat pies.

Signed Notso Humble MD 1 April 2007

Figure 10 – Sample food safety policy for Humble Meat Pies

5

Food safety management system planning

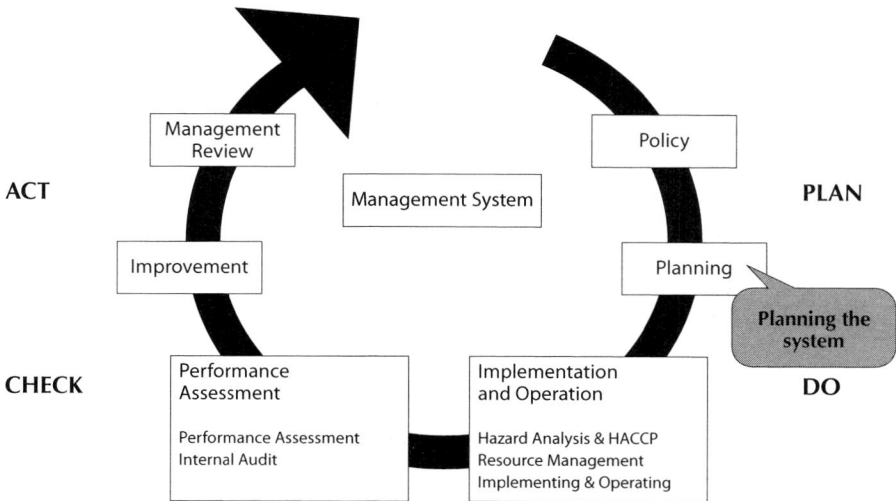

Figure 11 – Planning the system

This chapter, which focuses on planning, deals with hazard identification, legal requirements, contingency planning, objective setting and organizational structure. It relates specifically to the following clauses from ISO 22000:2005:

– Planning	5.3, 7.1
– Preliminary steps to enable hazard analysis	7.3.1, 7.3.2, 7.3.3, 7.3.5, 7.4, 7.6 (see Chapter 6)
– Legal and customer requirements	7.3.3.1, 7.2.2, 7.2.3
– Contingency planning	5.7, 7.10.4
– Objectives	5.1 (a), 5.2 (f), 5.3 (a), 8.2
– Organizational structure	5.4, 5.5, 7.10 (see Chapter 10)

From the outset, it is essential that there is commitment to food safety management at the highest level within and across the organization. Planning is fundamental to the successful implementation of a food safety management system. This is probably the most difficult stage of the process of implementation of ISO 22000:2005. Unless this stage is tackled comprehensively and effectively the whole system will have an inadequate foundation. Although planning is an integral part of all the elements of the system, ISO 22000 refers to the planning stage as follows:

> *Top management shall ensure that*
>
> a) *planning of the food safety management system is carried out to meet requirements given in 4.1 as well as the objectives of the organization that support food safety, and*
> b) *the integrity of the food safety management system is maintained when changes to the food safety management system are planned and implemented.*
>
> *(Clause 5.3)*

> *The organization shall plan and develop the processes needed for the realization of safe products...*
>
> *(Clause 7.1)*

Planning for a food safety management system is the same as planning for any other activity. It consists of:

- identifying specific requirements for the system – what needs to be done, where and in what priority;
- setting clear performance criteria – what needs to be done;
- identifying who is responsible – who will get it done and how;
- setting time-scales – when it is to be done by; and
- identifying the desired outcome – what should the result be.

The aim is to plan for a food safety management system capable of:

- effectively identifying, evaluating, controlling, monitoring and verifying food safety hazards in order to assure food safety;
- meeting the organization's food safety policy and objectives that support food safety;
- enabling effective communication internally and externally on food safety issues;
- managing potential emergency situations that can impact on food safety;
- reacting to changing demands – legal requirements, new technology, organizational changes, reaction to regulatory and customer requirements; and
- sustaining a positive food safety culture (see also Chapter 7).

ISO 22000 identifies the areas that need to be addressed which will be considered in turn.

5.1 Preliminary steps to enable hazard analysis

This is an essential element of the system. Most organizations working in the food sector will already be familiar with the process.

- All relevant information needed to conduct the hazard analysis needs to be collected, maintained, updated and documented (Clause 7.3.1) and a food safety team appointed (Clause 7.3.2).

- The food safety team has to conduct a hazard analysis to determine which hazards need to be controlled, the degree of control required to ensure food safety, and which combination of control measures is required (Clause 7.4.1).
- The operational prerequisite programmes need to be documented and include the following information for each programme: food safety hazards to be controlled by the programme, control measures, monitoring procedures that demonstrate that the operational PRPs are implemented, corrections and corrective actions to be taken if monitoring shows that the operational PRPs are not in control, responsibilities and authorities, records of monitoring (Clause 7.5).
- The HACCP plan has to be documented and include the following information for each identified critical control point: food safety hazards to be controlled at the CCP, control measures, critical limits, monitoring procedures, corrections and corrective actions to be taken if critical limits are exceeded, responsibilities and authorities, records of monitoring (Clause 7.6).
- Following the establishment of operational PRP(s) and/or the HACCP plan the organization needs to update the following information if necessary including product characteristics, intended use, flow diagrams, process steps, control measures (Clause 7.7).
- Verification planning needs to define the purpose, methods, frequencies and responsibilities for the verification activities (Clause 7.8).
- The organization needs to establish and apply a traceability system that enables the identification of product lots and their relation to batches of raw materials, processing and delivery records (Clause 7.9).
- Corrections: a documented procedure has to be established and maintained defining the identification and assessment of affected end products to determine their proper handling and a review of the corrections carried out (Clause 7.10).
- Corrective actions: the organization needs to establish and maintain documented procedures which specify appropriate actions to identify and eliminate the cause of detected nonconformities, to prevent recurrence, and to bring the process or system back into control after nonconformity has been encountered (Clause 7.10.2).

- The controls and related responses and authorization for dealing with potentially unsafe products have to be documented (Clause 7.10.3).
- The food safety team has to plan and implement the processes needed to validate control measures and/or control measure combinations, and to verify and improve the food safety management system (Clause 8.1).

Figure 2 in ISO/TS 22004 illustrates the steps in the planning of safe foods and shows how the steps addressed by the *Codex Alimentarius HACCP Guidelines* have been incorporated within ISO 22000 and the additional steps required by ISO 22000, establishing the operational prerequisite programmes (Clause 7.5) and validation of control measure combinations (Clause 8.2) (see Figure 15).

ISO/TS 22004, Clause 7 provides further guidance on planning for the realization of safe products.

For those who are developing a system without such arrangements in place this process is covered in detail in Chapter 6.

5.2 Legal and customer requirements

The organization needs to identify statutory and regulatory food safety requirements related to PRPs (Clause 7.2.2) and raw materials, ingredients and product-contact materials (Clause 7.3.3) and ensure that the food safety policy conforms with both statutory and regulatory requirements and with the mutually agreed food safety requirements of customers (Clause 5.2).

ISO 22000 also requires that 'When selecting and/or establishing PRPs, the organization shall consider and utilize appropriate information [e.g. statutory and regulatory requirements, customer requirements, recognized guidelines, Codex Alimentarius Commission (Codex) principles and codes of practice, national, international or sector standards]' (Clause 7.2.3).

The identification of legal requirements was dealt with in part in Chapter 2 (*Getting started*). A more comprehensive guide is given in Annex 2 with references to other sources of information which will enable the organization to identify current and forthcoming regulations that may apply.

5.3 Emergency preparedness and response

...establish, implement and maintain procedures to manage potential emergency situations and accidents that can impact food safety...

(Clause 5.7)

All organizations need to make arrangements for dealing with emergencies, whether it be fire evacuation or first aid. Food safety is no different in this respect.

Even very small organizations need to identify their risks of an emergency occurring and understand how they will address it. Equally, all organizations, large and small, need to have good continuity systems in place should there be a break in production or the business delivery system. Organizations should be aware of all potential emergency situations which may include fire, flooding, bioterrorism and sabotage, energy failure, vehicle accidents, contamination of the environment.

As well as assessing the risks posed by your own operations and practices, you need to be aware of hazards posed by neighbours that may affect your site. It is important to remember that emergency planning should go beyond evacuation and dealing with the incident. Organizations need to return to business as soon as possible, so they need to put in place plans for minimizing disruption following an emergency evacuation. Areas to be considered include:

– recovery of software for IT systems, ensuring secure storage, containment;
– safe recovery of undamaged plant and equipment from the original site;
– maintaining the FSMS at temporary sites; and
– reviewing the operation of the FSMS in the light of the emergency to identify and remedy any areas of failure so as to prevent a reoccurrence.

Checklist 7 is provided to assist in identifying the arrangements that should be in place. Tick yes if it has been addressed and no if arrangements are outstanding.

CHECKLIST 7 – Emergency preparedness

Yes	No	
❏	❏	Identify all potential emergencies that you could reasonably predict that might occur to your site (including your neighbour's).
❏	❏	Appoint a senior person to coordinate and liaise with external bodies.
❏	❏	Ensure procedures and equipment are in place for dealing with emergencies.
❏	❏	Train staff in evacuation and emergency procedures.
❏	❏	Notify emergency services of any risk they face.
❏	❏	Alert emergency services.
❏	❏	Evacuate staff and visitors.
❏	❏	Ensure there is contingency planning for remobilization after emergency.

A product which has reached the consumer market that is deficient in some way poses a major problem to those in the food supply industry. The logistics of dealing with faulty products is a considerable problem. Moreover, the withdrawal of the product is not the only major difficulty should this happen. It is now a legal requirement to notify consumers and regulatory bodies that an incident has occurred. In the event of an incident the following questions should be addressed:

–   What is the nature of the problem?
–   How much product has been affected?
–   How far into the marketplace has it been distributed?
–   What steps should be taken to isolate and recall?
–   What public notification should be issued and to whom?
–   How is the cause of the problem to be rectified?

> ...Withdrawn products shall be secured or held under supervision until they are destroyed, used for purposes other than originally intended, determined to be safe for the same (or other) intended use, or reprocessed in a manner to ensure they become safe.
>
> The cause, extent and result of a withdrawal shall be recorded and reported to top management as input to the management review...

The organization shall verify and record the effectiveness of the withdrawal programme through the use of appropriate techniques (e.g. mock withdrawal or practice withdrawal).

(Clause 7.10.4)

Checklist 8 is provided to assist you to identify if the necessary arrangements are in place.

CHECKLIST 8 – Arrangements for product withdrawal

Yes	No	
❏	❏	Has the organization established contingency arrangements for product withdrawal?
❏	❏	Has the organization set up a communication system with its customers in the case of such an emergency?
❏	❏	Have there been any trial runs?
❏	❏	Have lessons been learned from real events and trial runs and corrective action taken?
❏	❏	Have top management appointed personnel with the authority to initiate a withdrawal?
❏	❏	Have top management appointed personnel responsible for executing the withdrawal?
❏	❏	Has a documented procedure been produced for notification to relevant interested parties?
❏	❏	Has a documented procedure been produced for handling the withdrawal of products?
❏	❏	Has a documented procedure been produced for dealing with affected products in stock?
❏	❏	Does the procedure identify the sequence of events that need to be initiated?

5.4 Establishing objectives and targets

The initial part of the planning process involves setting objectives. The primary sources of information for this will primarily come from the initial status review (the getting started stage: see Chapter 2), the hazard analysis (Chapter 6) and the management review (Chapter 13) and business issues.

Objectives and targets may include identification and implementation of activities to improve any aspect of the food safety system. Examples of objectives are:

–   *improve* the traceability system;
–   *reduce* the number of withdrawals/recalls;
–   *introduce* an emergency preparedness and response plan;
–   *introduce* a plan for external communication on food safety issues;
–   *reduce* the number of occasions when critical limits are exceeded;
–   *eliminate* microbiological contamination at process step X; and
–   *maintain microbiological loading in chilled raw materials at level X.*

At a later stage, these plans may be revised in the light of outputs from management reviews. The objectives should be relevant to the business and not just added for the sake of it. It is important to remember that objectives are not cast in tablets of stone and should evolve as the management system develops and matures.

The objectives should be SMART objectives i.e. specific, measurable, achievable, relevant and time bound. Objectives should describe what is to be achieved, e.g. the training and development of all employees responsible for monitoring, corrections and corrective actions, the completion of the hazard analysis covering all processes of the organization. They will assign performance criteria – delivery targets and deadlines and responsibilities for delivery, from top management down through the organization – and provide a mechanism for escalation of food safety management issues up through the organization.

The organization should establish and maintain a food safety management programme for achieving its objectives (see Figure 12). This should include documentation of:

–   the designated responsibility and authority for achievement of the objectives at relevant functions and levels of the organization; and
–   the means and time-scale by which objectives are to be achieved.

This programme should be reviewed at regular and planned intervals to address changes to the activities, products, services or operating conditions of the organization to ensure:

- overall plans and objectives, including employees and resources, for the organization to implement its policy;
- operational plans to implement arrangements to control the hazards identified;
- contingency plans for foreseeable emergencies and to mitigate their effects (e.g. prevention, preparedness and response procedures);
- planning for organizational activities;
- plans covering the management of change of either a permanent or temporary nature (e.g. associated with new processes or plant, working procedures, production fluctuations, legal requirements, organizational and staffing changes);
- plans covering interactions with other interested parties (e.g. control, selection and management of suppliers and customers, liaison with emergency services);
- planning for measuring performance, audits and status reviews; and
- implementing corrective actions;

5.5 Organizational structure

The organization needs to identify who is responsible and accountable for the provision of the food safety management system. This can be in the form of an organization chart and job descriptions. The identification of the FSTL has been addressed. Prime responsibility lies with top management.

It is important that all those involved in the organization's food process understand their individual responsibilities and the impact that they can have if they do not exercise the correct controls. If the commitment and culture of the organization are poor, then the likelihood of failure is greater. The issue of creating an effective climate for achieving organizational commitment is dealt with in Chapter 7.

Number	Description of objective	Target to be achieved	Time-scale for completion	Method for achieving objective and target	Responsibility for managing implementation of objective	Tracking of progress to achieve objective
1	Reduce the number of foreign-body complaints received on metal shavings from 100 complaints a year	by 50%	By end of 2007	Awareness training of all staff in production, cleaning and engineering on methods to avoid metal contamination	Production manager	Monthly basis by the FSTL

Figure 12 – Example of measurable objective and target

Clear reporting lines need to be established, and ISO 22000 states:

Responsibility and authority

Top management shall ensure that responsibilities and authorities are defined and communicated within the organization to ensure the effective operation and maintenance of the food safety management system.

All personnel shall have responsibility to report problems with the food safety management system to identified person(s). Designated personnel shall have defined responsibility and authority to initiate and record actions.

(Clause 5.4)

Once the system is established to deliver the above areas, there need to be plans for ensuring that the system is operating effectively and is improved through validation, verification, audit and management review, and so on.

Checklist 9 identifies the main areas that need to be addressed. Tickboxes are provided for you to identify those procedures you already have in place (1) and those that you need to introduce (2).

CHECKLIST 9 – Areas that need to be addressed

1	2	
❏	❏	Prepare overall plans and objectives for achieving food safety policy.
❏	❏	Define responsibilities and authorities for the FSTL and food safety team.
❏	❏	Ensure sufficient knowledge, skills and experience in the organization to manage food safety issues effectively.
❏	❏	Arrangements for communication on food safety issues with other parties – contractors, suppliers, customers, regulatory authorities, consumers.
❏	❏	Arrangements for communication on food safety issues within the organization.
❏	❏	Programme for collection, maintenance and updating of all relevant information for conducting hazard analyses.
❏	❏	Programme for hazard identification, assessment and selection of control measures.
❏	❏	Prerequisite programme for implementing operational control of food safety hazards.
❏	❏	HACCP plan for implementing operational control of food safety hazards.
❏	❏	Validation activity plan – control measures.
❏	❏	Verification activity plan – audits, product testing, evaluation and analysis of results.

1	2	
❏	❏	Arrangements for emergency preparedness and response.
❏	❏	Traceability programme.
❏	❏	Plan for control of nonconformities – corrections, corrective actions, handling of potentially unsafe product.
❏	❏	Arrangements for handling withdrawal of product.
❏	❏	Arrangements for updating the food safety management system.
❏	❏	Identification of legal and customer requirements.
❏	❏	Identification of applicable information for selecting/establishing PRPs – Codex, sector standards, codes of practice.
❏	❏	Arrangements for conducting management reviews.

6

Hazard analysis and the HACCP programme

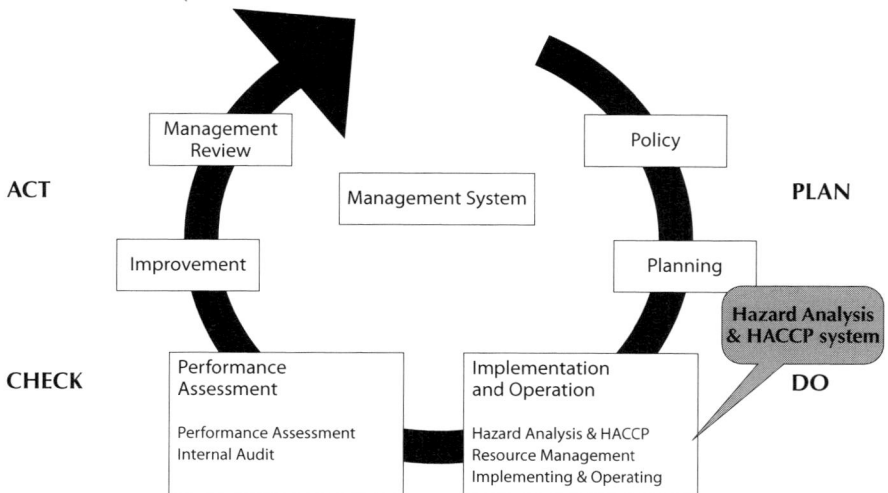

Figure 13 – Hazard analysis and HACCP system

This chapter is about hazard analysis, preparation of HACCP plans and pre-requisites and operational prerequisite programmes for implementation and planning for verification. It relates specifically to the following clause from ISO 22000:2005:

– Planning and realization of safe products	Clause 7 (specifically 7.6.5 and 7.9)

6.1 HACCP principles

Assessments of the food safety hazards and their associated risks to consumers, and the development and implementation of controls to prevent, reduce or eliminate such hazards are the basis of an effective food safety management system.

In the UK, the hygiene regulations require that food safety procedures are developed on the basis of HACCP principles. HACCP is defined as a system which identifies, evaluates and controls hazards which are significant for food safety (*Codex Alimentarius, Recommended International Code of Practice – General Principles of Food Hygiene*).

ISO 22000 uses a systematic approach for the development of pre-requisite programmes and HACCP plans by integrating the seven principles of HACCP and application steps set out in the Codex Alimentarius Commission code of practice.

The seven HACCP principles are:

1 conduct a hazard analysis;
2 determine the critical control points (CCPs);
3 establish critical limits;
4 establish a system to monitor control of the CCP;
5 establish the corrective action to be taken when monitoring indicates that a particular CCP is not under control;

6   establish procedures for verification to confirm that the HACCP system is working effectively; and
7   establish documentation concerning all procedures and records appropriate to these principles and their application.

ISO 22000 also incorporates the 'preliminary steps' set out by Codex which are five activities or steps that need to be completed before the hazard analysis can be started. The purpose of the preliminary steps is to collect the necessary information on product characteristics (raw materials, ingredients, product-contact materials, end products, intended use) and processes for which the hazard analysis is to be conducted as well as put in place a food safety team that has the experience, knowledge and skills to conduct the hazard analysis. The logical sequence for the 12 application steps for HACCP is illustrated in Figure 14.

ISO 22000 gives correspondence between HACCP principles, HACCP application steps and the relevant clause of ISO 22000 (see Table 1).

Logic sequence for application of HACCP (12 steps) **Seven principles of the HACCP system**

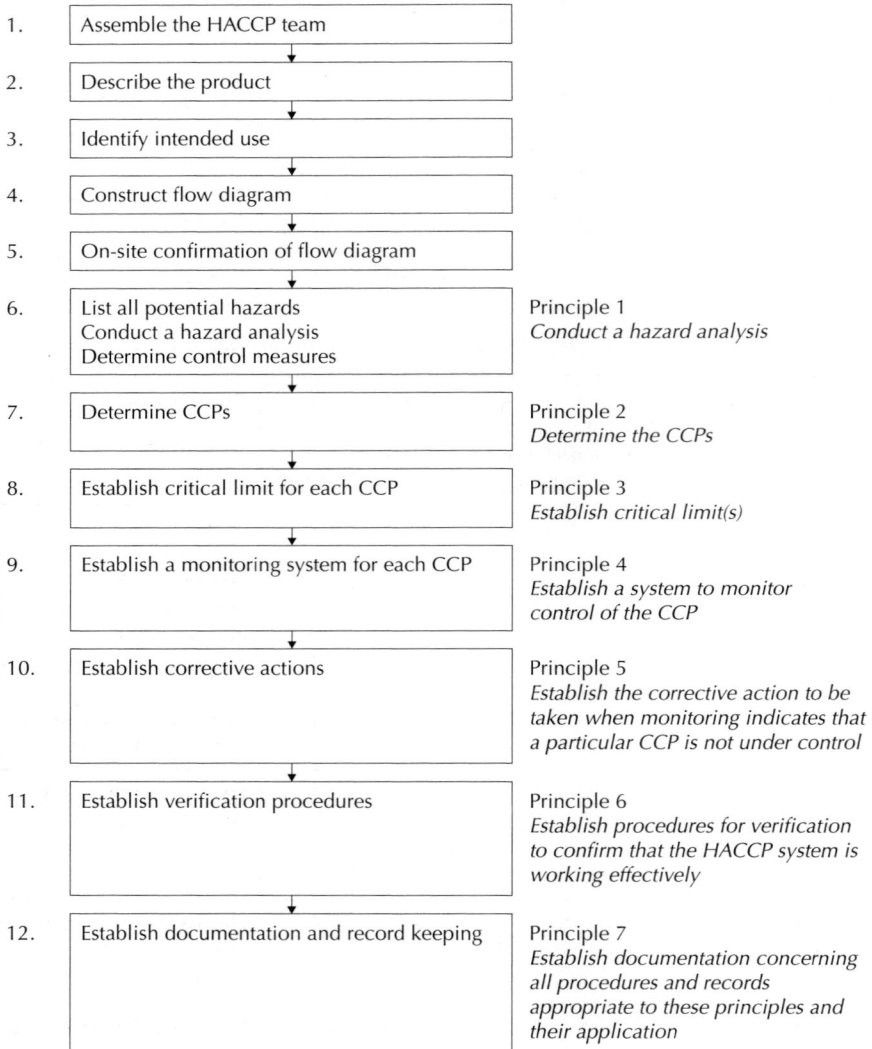

1.	Assemble the HACCP team
2.	Describe the product
3.	Identify intended use
4.	Construct flow diagram
5.	On-site confirmation of flow diagram

6. List all potential hazards / Conduct a hazard analysis / Determine control measures — **Principle 1** *Conduct a hazard analysis*

7. Determine CCPs — **Principle 2** *Determine the CCPs*

8. Establish critical limit for each CCP — **Principle 3** *Establish critical limit(s)*

9. Establish a monitoring system for each CCP — **Principle 4** *Establish a system to monitor control of the CCP*

10. Establish corrective actions — **Principle 5** *Establish the corrective action to be taken when monitoring indicates that a particular CCP is not under control*

11. Establish verification procedures — **Principle 6** *Establish procedures for verification to confirm that the HACCP system is working effectively*

12. Establish documentation and record keeping — **Principle 7** *Establish documentation concerning all procedures and records appropriate to these principles and their application*

Figure 14 – The relationship between the 7 principles and the 12 steps of HACCP in Codex Alimentarius

Table 1 – Cross references between the HACCP principles and application steps and clauses of ISO 22000:2005

Source: ISO 22000:2005, Table B.1

HACCP Principles	HACCP application steps		ISO 22000:2005	
	Assemble HACCP team	Step 1	7.3.2	Food safety team
	Describe product	Step 2	7.3.3	Product characteristics
			7.3.5.2	Description of process steps and control measures
	Identify intended use	Step 3	7.3.4	Intended use
	Construct flow diagram	Step 4	7.3.5.1	Flow diagrams
	On-site confirmation of flow diagram	Step 5		
Principle 1 Conduct a hazard analysis.	List all potential hazards	Step 6	7.4	Hazard analysis
	Conduct a hazard analysis		7.4.2	Hazard identification and determination of acceptable levels
	Consider control measures		7.4.3	Hazard assessment
			7.4.4	Selection and assessment of control measures
Principle 2 Determine the critical control points (CCPs).	Determine CCPs	Step 7	7.6.2	Identification of critical control points (CCPs)
Principle 3 Establish critical limit(s).	Establish critical limits for each CCP	Step 8	7.6.3	Determination of critical limits for critical control points
Principle 4 Establish a system to monitor control of the CCP.	Establish a monitoring system for each CCP	Step 9	7.6.4	System for the monitoring of critical control points

Principle 5 Establish the corrective action to be taken when monitoring indicates that a particular CCP is not under control.	Establish corrective actions	Step 10	7.6.5	Actions when monitoring results exceed critical limits
Principle 6 Establish procedures for verification to confirm that the HACCP system is working effectively.	Establish verification procedures	Step 11	7.8	Verification planning
Principle 7 Establish documentation concerning all procedures and records appropriate to these principles and their application.	Establish documentation and record keeping	Step 12	4.2 7.7	Documentation requirements Updating of preliminary information and documents specifying the PRPs and the HACCP plan

6.2 Terminology

Before commencing an implementation programme it is necessary to familiarize yourself with the specific terminology used in the ISO 22000 standard.

6.2.1 Control measures

Traditionally, control measures have been divided into two groups, but the ISO 22000 standard groups these control measures into three areas: prerequisite programmes (PRPs), operational prerequisite programmes (operational PRPs) and an HACCP plan incorporating critical control points

(CCPs). A further explanation of these terms is provided in ISO/TS 22004 as detailed below:

a) *prerequisite programmes (PRPs) that manage the basic conditions and activities; the PRPs are not selected for the purpose of controlling specific identified hazards but for the purpose of maintaining a hygienic production, processing and/or handling environment;*

b) *operational prerequisite programmes (operational PRPs) that manage those control measures that the hazard analysis identifies as necessary to control identified hazards to acceptable levels, and which are not otherwise managed by the HACCP plan;*

c) *a HACCP plan to manage those control measures that the hazard analysis identifies as necessary to control hazards to acceptable levels, and which are applied at critical control points (CCPs).*

(ISO/TS 22004, Clause 7.1)

6.2.2 Verification vs. Validation

Application of the step of 'verification' in Codex is defined as being made up of two activities: validation and verification. ISO 22000 categorizes these two activities as separate and distinct.

Validation is defined as 'obtaining evidence that the control measures managed by the HACCP plan and by the operational PRPs are capable of being effective' (Clause 3.15), i.e. before implementation of the HACCP plan or PRPs.

Verification is defined as 'confirmation, through the provision of objective evidence, that specified requirements have been fulfilled' (Clause 3.16). As can be seen from Figure 15, validation is shown as a separate activity from verification in the process for developing HACCP plans and PRPs.

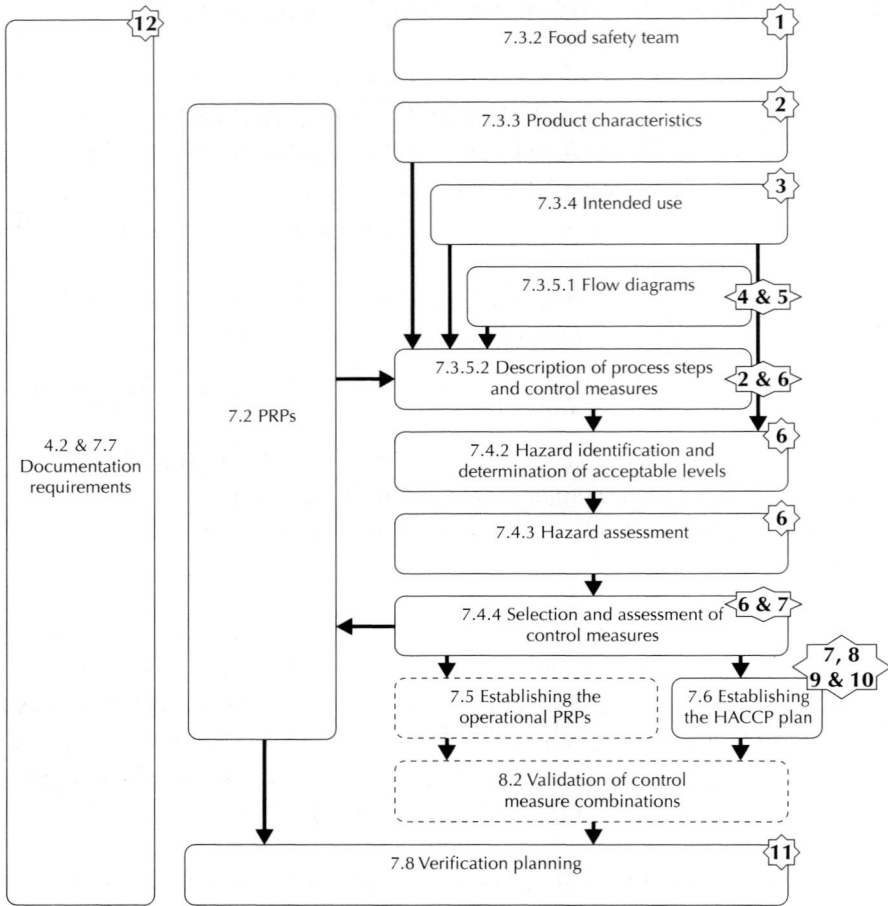

Key

⬡ Steps addressed by the *Codex Alimentarius* HACCP guidelines

⌐⌐⌐ Steps specific to ISO 22000

NOTE Cross-references refer to ISO 22000:2005.

Source: ISO/TS 22004:2006, Figure 2

Figure 15 – Planning of safe foods

ISO 22000 defines prerequisite programmes as

> *basic conditions and activities that are necessary to maintain a hygienic environment throughout the food chain suitable for the production, handling and provision of safe end products and safe food for human consumption*
>
> *(Clause 3.8)*

Clause 7.2 requires that PRPs are established, implemented and maintained to help in controlling:

- likelihood of introducing food safety hazards to the product through the work environment;
- biological, chemical and physical contamination of the products, including cross-contamination between products; and
- food safety hazard levels in the product and product processing environment.

When considering PRPs, there are a range of food safety issues that apply to many organizations. ISO 22000 requires that in selecting PRPs, consideration should be given to using appropriate information (e.g. statutory and regulatory requirements, customer requirements). The following list with brief descriptors, while not necessarily exhaustive, should provide a guide for consideration to complement those set out in ISO 22000:2005, Clause 7.2.3.

- *Premises and facilities* – a programme is required to ensure that the layout, construction and facilities within your premises meet legal requirements and take account of good practice guidelines with respect to, for example, minimizing cross-contamination or preventing the introduction of food safety hazards. This programme should not only evaluate the premises at the start, but should manage any changes and any ongoing maintenance.
- *Personal hygiene* – the personal hygiene of staff is of major importance to food safety, as people are a source of and/or a vehicle for food safety hazards. There should be a programme which communicates

the requirements and monitors compliance in respect of personal cleanliness, hand washing, personal habits (e.g. smoking), health/fitness for work and the wearing of protective clothing.

- *Pest control* – food businesses must have adequate procedures to prevent access to the premises by pests and domestic pets and control infestations. This may be carried out by a pest control contractor, but it is the responsibility of the business to manage and monitor this contract and ensure that the contractor is diligent in their monitoring and corrective actions, and that they are acting in accordance with the law (particularly in relation to baits and chemicals). A failure on the part of a contractor will still be a non-compliance with regard to the business.
- *Sanitation and cleaning* – all aspects of the premises must be appropriately cleaned and disinfected on a regular basis. This includes food contact surfaces, equipment and utensils, as well as the internal fabric of the food area itself. A well-organized cleaning programme covering all areas at appropriate frequencies is required, along with the careful storage, handling and use of cleaning chemicals to control risk of chemical contamination.
- *Waste management* – this programme is often incorporated with the sanitation and cleaning programme, but if so, care must be taken to ensure that the handling and disposal of waste during food preparation and service is included rather than just waste disposal during cleaning.
- *Raw materials and ingredients* – this programme must control and monitor the supply of raw materials to your business to ensure that you do not accept anything that might contaminate or pose a food safety risk to your food products. In addition, this programme must control the storage, handling, stock rotation and re-use of ingredients or components with particular regard to the introduction of contaminants and any temperature control requirements.
- *Maintenance and servicing* – this programme should be in place to manage the maintenance and any required calibration of equipment within the food preparation and service operation, including equipment that is not directly used for preparation but the malfunction of

which could have food safety implications, e.g. ventilation systems, temperature probes.

– *Foreign object control* – this programme should evaluate, monitor and control any potential foreign object risks that are not covered by other PRPs, such as regular checks on any glass/hard plastic items and rules governing the use of hazardous items such as paper clips or pens with separate caps.

– *Packing and transport* – if you deliver your products to your customer, a programme to evaluate, control and monitor food safety hazards arising from the wrapping, transport containers and vehicles must be in place.

6.2.3 Other aspects for consideration

In addition to the food safety-specific PRPs, there are further elements which support the HACCP system which it may be useful to consider as PRPs in their own right, particularly if you have a separate quality system already in place within your organization. While it is not essential to have these set up as PRPs, they are issues which must be addressed within your food safety management system.

– *Document control* – a set of procedures governing the update, replacement and tracking of all documents (whether external or developed internally) within your HACCP system should be considered. Where documents are produced and kept electronically, care must be taken not to simply revise or overwrite the existing file, as past documents will be required for evidence of due diligence where legal compliance is questioned. A list of documented procedures, records and statements required by ISO 22000 are set out in Chapter 9.

– *Traceability* – a system which tracks the source and destination of all materials and ingredients used in your food is a legal requirement. A system which records the batch/lot details of all ingredients/raw materials and monitors/records their use should be maintained.

Have you addressed the following in Checklist 10 which ISO 22000:2005 (Clause 7.2.3) requires to be considered when developing PRPs?

CHECKLIST 10 – Considerations for developing PRPs

Yes	No	
☐	☐	Construction and layout of buildings and associated utilities
☐	☐	Layout of premises, including workspace and employee facilities
☐	☐	Supplies of air, water, energy and other utilities
☐	☐	Supporting services including waste and waste disposal
☐	☐	Suitability of equipment and its accessibility for cleaning, maintenance and preventative maintenance
☐	☐	Management of purchased materials (e.g. raw materials, ingredients, chemicals and packaging), supplies (e.g. water, air steam and ice), disposals (e.g. waste and sewage) and handling of products (e.g. storage and transportation)
☐	☐	Measures for preventing cross-contamination
☐	☐	Personal hygiene
☐	☐	Pest control
☐	☐	Cleaning and sanitizing
☐	☐	Other aspects as appropriate, e.g. document control, traceability, withdrawals

The process described below for developing HACCP plans and prerequisite programmes follows a logical approach as set out in Figure 15, and shows the correspondence between the ISO 22000 clauses and the *Codex Alimentarius HACCP Guidelines*. As you will see from the illustration ISO 22000 introduces two steps that are in addition to Codex; operational prerequisite programmes and validation of control measures.

6.3 Preliminary steps to enable hazard analysis

All relevant information needed to conduct the hazard analysis shall be collected, maintained, updated and documented. Records shall be maintained.

(Clause 7.3.1)

6.3.1 Food safety team (Codex HACCP application step 1)

ISO 22000 states:

> A food safety team shall be appointed.
> The food safety team shall have a combination of multi-disciplinary knowledge and experience in developing and implementing the food safety management system. This includes, but need not be limited to, the organization's products, processes, equipment and food safety hazards within the scope of the food safety management system...
>
> *(Clause 7.3.2)*

The food safety team should be appropriate for the size, complexity and risk of the organization. The size of an organization may dictate the availability of a team that has the combined multidisciplinary knowledge and experience needed and so consideration may have to be given to accessing external advisers to the organization. The food safety team as a whole should have the knowledge and experience to be able to conduct the hazard analysis and could, for example, include engineers, technical managers, microbiologists, personnel in receiving, processing, packaging, and so on.

Checklist 11 identifies the key areas for appointing the food safety team. Tickboxes are provided for you to identify those areas you already have in place (1) and those you may need to introduce (2).

CHECKLIST 11 – Appointing a food safety team

Yes	No	
❑	❑	The responsibilities of the food safety team have been defined and recorded, e.g. development of the HACCP plan for X, Y, Z products or product groupings
❑	❑	A team with the multidisciplinary knowledge and experience has been appointed
❑	❑	A record of the knowledge and experience of the food safety team members has been established

6.3.2 Product characteristics (Codex HACCP application step 2)

Product characteristics include descriptions of raw materials, ingredients, product-contact materials and end products. ISO 22000 provides the following list of issues that must be considered.

> *All raw materials, ingredients and product-contact materials shall be described in documents to the extent needed to conduct the hazard analysis... including the following, as appropriate:*
>
> a)   *biological, chemical and physical characteristics;*
> b)   *composition of formulated ingredients, including additives and processing aids;*
> c)   *origin;*
> d)   *method of production;*
> e)   *packaging and delivery methods;*
> f)   *storage conditions and shelf life;*
> g)   *preparation and/or handling before use or processing;*
> h)   *food safety-related acceptance criteria or specifications of purchased materials and ingredients appropriate to their intended uses.*
>
> *The organization shall identify statutory and regulatory food safety requirements related to the above.*
>   *The descriptions shall be kept up-to-date including, when required...*
>
> (Clause 7.3.3.1)
>
> *The characteristics of end products shall be described in documents to the extent needed to conduct the hazard analysis... including information on the following as appropriate:*
>
> a)   *product name or similar identification;*
> b)   *composition;*

c) biological, chemical and physical characteristics relevant for food safety;
d) intended shelf life and storage conditions;
e) packaging;
f) labelling relating to food safety and/or instructions for handling, preparation and usage;
g) method(s) of distribution.

The organization shall identify statutory and regulatory food safety requirements related to the above.
   The descriptions shall be kept up-to-date...

(Clause 7.3.3.2)

Description of process steps and control measures
The existing control measures, process parameters and/or the rigorousness with which they are applied, or procedures that may influence food safety, shall be described to the extent needed to conduct the hazard analysis...
   External requirements...that may impact the choice and the rigorousness of the control measures shall also be described...

(Clause 7.3.5.2)

6.3.3 Intended use (Codex HACCP application step 3)

ISO 22000 states:

The intended use, the reasonably expected handling of the end product, and any unintended but reasonably expected mishandling and misuse of the end product shall be considered...
   Groups of users and, where appropriate, groups of consumers shall be identified for each product, and consumer groups known to be especially vulnerable to specific food safety hazards shall be considered...

(Clause 7.3.4)

Consideration should be given to:

- how the product is intended to be used;
- who will consume the food and whether any of the consumer groups are vulnerable groups, e.g. babies, sick people; and
- how the food is to be handled, e.g. refrigerated, cooked before consumption.

6.3.4 Flow diagrams, process steps and control measures (Codex HACCP application steps 4 and 5)

The use of flow diagrams as a representation of the products or processes covered by the food safety management system is a specific requirement of the standard. The initial approach will be to identify inputs and outputs for each step in the process recognizing that the output from one step in the process may form the input to another process (see Figure 16).

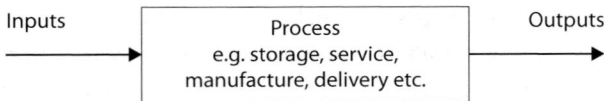

Figure 16 – Input/output relationship

ISO 22000 states:

> *Flow diagrams shall be prepared for the products or process categories covered by the food safety management system…*
> *Flow diagrams shall be clear, accurate and sufficiently detailed. Flow diagrams shall, as appropriate, include the following:*
>
> a) *the sequence and interaction of all steps in the operation;*
> b) *any outsourced processes and subcontracted work;*
> c) *where raw materials, ingredients and intermediate products enter the flow;*

d)   *where reworking and recycling take place;*

e)   *where end products, intermediate products, by-products and waste are released or removed...*

(Clause 7.3.5.1)

Once the flow diagram has been defined, including the points a) to e) above, then the food safety team must verify its accuracy and keep a record of this verification. The record will form an accurate basis for identifying the food safety hazards at each step of the process during the hazard analysis.

Additionally, there is a legal requirement for the traceability of food on a 'one-step-up and one-step-down' basis and the correctly documented flow charts should include details of the product ingredient, e.g. supplier, dates, batch numbers, and so on. This is also a requirement of Clause 7.9 (see below).

Traceability system

The organization shall establish and apply a traceability system that enables the identification of product lots and their relation to batches of raw materials, processing and delivery records.

The traceability system shall be able to identify incoming material from the immediate suppliers and the initial distribution route of the end product.

Traceability records shall be maintained for a defined period for system assessment to enable the handling of potentially unsafe products and in the event of product withdrawal. Records shall be in accordance with statutory and regulatory requirements and customer requirements and may, for example, be based on the end product lot identification.

(Clause 7.9)

Figure 17 is an example of a flow diagram that illustrates the sequence and interaction of the process steps and where raw materials, ingredients and intermediate products enter the flow and process control parameters, e.g. temperatures in the production of baked chicken Kiev in a catering facility.

1. Raw chicken breast　　2. Butter　　　　3. Garlic puree　　8. Raw egg　　9. Breadcrumbs
　　　　　　　　　　　　　　　　　　　　4. Chopped parsley
　　　　　　　　　　　　　　　　　　　　5. Lemon juice
　　　　　　　　　　　　　　　　　　　　6. Pepper
　　　　　　　　　　　　　　　　　　　　7. Salt

10. Store 2–5°C　　　11. Store 2–5°C　　12. Ambient　　13. Store 2–5°C　　14. Ambient

15. Slice pocket　　　16. Mix butter, garlic puree, parsley,　　17. Beat in bowl
　　in chicken　　　　　　lemon juice, pepper & salt in bowl

18. Stuff with garlic butter mix

19. Coat with egg

20. Coat with breadcrumbs

21. Place on tray

22. Place in oven temp 200°C for 35 min

23. Transfer to hot holding at minimum of 63°C

24. Transfer to plate and serve to customer

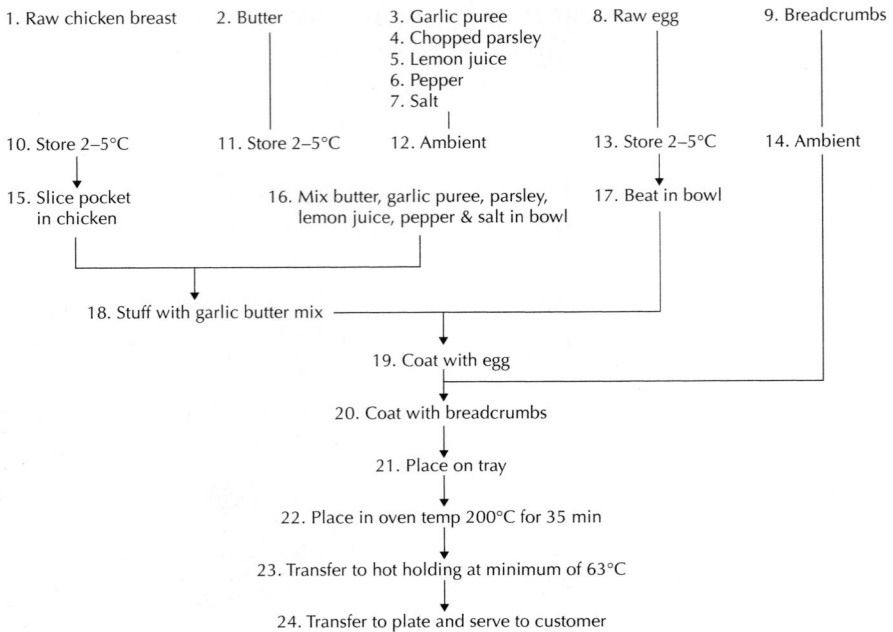

Issue: (date) (issue no.)　　　　　　　　　　　　　　Signed:

*Figure 17 – Example of a schematic flow
diagram for baked chicken Kiev*

6.4 Hazard analysis – development of HACCP plans and PRPs

This section deals with the seven HACCP principles and their relationship to the twelve application steps (see Table 1).

6.4.1 Hazard analysis (Codex principle 1 and HACCP application step 6)

Once the flow diagrams have been defined and verified for accuracy, the hazard analysis can then be conducted to identify hazards that could reasonably be expected to occur at each step of the process flow chart.
ISO 22000 states:

> *The food safety team shall conduct a hazard analysis to determine which hazards need to be controlled, the degree of control required to ensure food safety, and which combination of control measures is required.*
>
> *(Clause 7.4.1)*

> *All food safety hazards that are reasonably expected to occur in relation to the type of product, type of process and actual processing facilities shall be identified and recorded…*
>
> *The step(s) (from raw materials, processing and distribution) at which each food safety hazard may be introduced shall be indicated.*
>
> *(Clause 7.4.2.1)*

The ongoing nature of the 'one-step-up one-step-down' principle is further reinforced in the standard:

> *When identifying the hazards, consideration shall be given to*
>
> *a)   the steps preceding and following the specified operation,*
> *b)   the process equipment, utilities/services and surroundings, and*
> *c)   the preceding and following links in the food chain.*
>
> *(Clause 7.4.2.2)*

> *For each of the food safety hazards identified, the acceptable level of the food safety hazard in the end product shall be determined whenever possible. The determined level shall take into account established statutory and regulatory requirements, customer food*

safety requirements, the intended use by the customer...The
justification for, and the result of, the determination shall be recorded.
(Clause 7.4.2.3)

ISO/TS 22004, Clause 7.4.2 gives guidance on determining acceptable levels of the food safety hazard in the end product and states the following:

Where statutory and regulatory authorities have established maximum limits, objectives, targets or end product and/or process criteria for a specific hazard–product combination, the hazard in question automatically becomes relevant for that product.

The 'acceptable level' means the level of a particular hazard in the end product of the organization that is needed at the next step in the food chain to ensure food safety; it refers to the acceptable level in foods for direct consumption only when the next step is actual consumption. The acceptable level in the end product should be determined through information obtained from one or more of the sources below:

a) *objectives, targets...or end product criteria established by statutory and regulatory authorities in the country of sale;*

b) *specifications ...or other information communicated by the organization constituting the subsequent step in the food chain (often the customer), in particular for end products intended for further processing or use other than direct consumption;*

c) *the maximum levels found acceptable by the food safety team, taking into account acceptable levels agreed on with the customer and/or established by law and, in the absence ...through scientific literature and professional experience.*
(ISO/TS 22004, Clause 7.4.2)

A hazard assessment shall be conducted to determine, for each food safety hazard identified... whether its elimination or reduction to acceptable levels is essential to the production of a safe food...

> *Each food safety hazard shall be evaluated according to the possible severity of adverse health effects and the likelihood of their occurrence. The methodology used shall be described, and the results of the food safety hazard assessment shall be recorded.*
>
> *(ISO 22000, Clause 7.4.3)*

An example of a food safety risk assessment matrix is set out in Figure 18.

Frequency						
Unlikely **(1)**	**Seldom** **(2)**	**Occasional** **(3)**	**Likely** **(4)**	**Frequent** **(5)**		
1	2	3	4	5	**Negligible** **(1)**	
2	4	6	8	10	**Moderate** **(2)**	**Severity**
3	6	9	12	15	**Critical** **(3)**	
4	8	12	16	20	**Catastrophic** **(4)**	

Key: ☐ Low Risk ☐ Medium Risk ■ High Risk ■ Extremely High Risk

Severity
- *Catastrophic* – Complete business failure due to food product contamination resulting in deaths.
- *Critical* – Major business impact due to food product contamination resulting in severe illnesses.
- *Moderate* – Minor business impact due to food product contamination resulting in minor illnesses.
- *Negligible* – Virtually no business impact nor illnesses.

Probability
- *Frequent* – Occurs often to individual and customer is continually exposed.
- *Likely* – Occurs several times and customers are exposed regularly.
- *Occasional* – Will occur and occurs sporadically in population.
- *Seldom* – May occur and occurs seldom in a customer.
- *Unlikely* – So unlikely you can assume it will not occur and occurs very rarely in population.

Figure 18 – An example of a food safety risk assessment matrix

The purpose of the hazard assessment is to evaluate the list of hazards that have been identified and to determine the hazards that need to be controlled. While not exhaustive, the hazard analysis should include the following points:

– source of the hazard;
– how the hazard could be introduced into the product;
– likely occurrence of hazards and severity and their ill effects;
– qualitative and/or quantitative evaluation of the presence of hazards;
– survival or multiplication of micro-organisms of concern;
– production or persistence in foods of toxins, chemicals or physical agents; and
– conditions leading to any of the above.

Di Longcroft's Residential Conference Centre, Holbeton
DLRCC found the process of hazard identification very demanding, as they were such a new organization. There were apparently so many control points. They found that by using a simple matrix such as the one above they were able to identify quickly those that they could discount, allowing them to concentrate on hazards that needed a greater level of control.

It may well be that more than one control measure is appropriate and therefore ISO 22000 requires that:

> ...an appropriate combination of control measures shall be selected which is capable of preventing, eliminating or reducing these food safety hazards to defined acceptable levels...
>
> *(Clause 7.4.4)*

It is a requirement that control measures are categorized in a logical manner to determine the manner in which they can best be managed:

The control measures selected shall be categorized as to whether they need to be managed through operational PRP(s) or by the HACCP plan...

...using a logical approach...

(Clause 7.4.4)

ISO 22000 sets out seven assessments that must be carried out when selecting and categorizing control measures. The results of the assessments carried out must be recorded, and a description of the methodology and parameters used for categorizing the control measures must be documented.

...The selection and categorization shall be carried out using a logical approach that includes assessments with regard to the following:

a) *its effect on identified food safety hazards relative to the strictness applied;*

b) *its feasibility for monitoring...;*

c) *its place within the system relative to other control measures;*

d) *the likelihood of failure in the functioning of a control measure or significant processing variability;*

e) *the severity of the consequence(s) in the case of failure in its functioning;*

f) *whether the control measure is specially established and applied to eliminate or significantly reduce the level of hazard(s);*

g) *synergistic effects (i.e. interaction that occurs between two or more measures resulting in their combined effect being higher than the sum of their individual effects)...*

(Clause 7.4.4)

If control measures are categorized as belonging to the HACCP plan then these control measures must be implemented according to the requirement of an HACCP plan set out in Clause 7.6. If control measures are categorized as belonging to the operational prerequisite programme, then these control measures must be implemented according to the requirement of operational prerequisite programmes set out in Clause 7.5.

Further guidance on the selection, assessment, categorization and combination of control measures is given in ISO/TS 22004, Clause 7.4.4.

6.4.2 Identification of critical control points (Codex principle 2 and HACCP application step 7)

Once the analysis stage is completed and it has been determined by which mechanism the control measures are to be managed – operational PRPs or HACCP plan as above – it is necessary to identify critical control points (CCPs). ISO 22000 states:

> For each hazard that is to be controlled by the HACCP plan, CCP(s) shall be identified for the control measures identified...
>
> *(Clause 7.6.2)*

There are a number of different approaches or decision trees that can be used to identify CCPs. One example is the decision tree set out in *Codex Alimentarius, Recommended International Code of Practice – General Principles of Food Hygiene* (see Figure 19).

Another approach can be found in ISO/TS 22004 which sets out a process which may be used to identify the control measures needed and whether the control measures will sit within the HACCP plan or the operational prerequisite programmes (see Figure 20).

6.4.3 Determination of critical limits for CCPs (Codex principle 3 and HACCP application step 8)

ISO 22000 states:

> Critical limits shall be determined for the monitoring established for each CCP...
>
> Critical limits shall be measurable.

The rationale for the...critical limits shall be documented.
Critical limits based on subjective data (such as visual inspection
of product, process, handling, etc.) shall be supported by
instructions...and/or education and training.

(Clause 7.6.3).

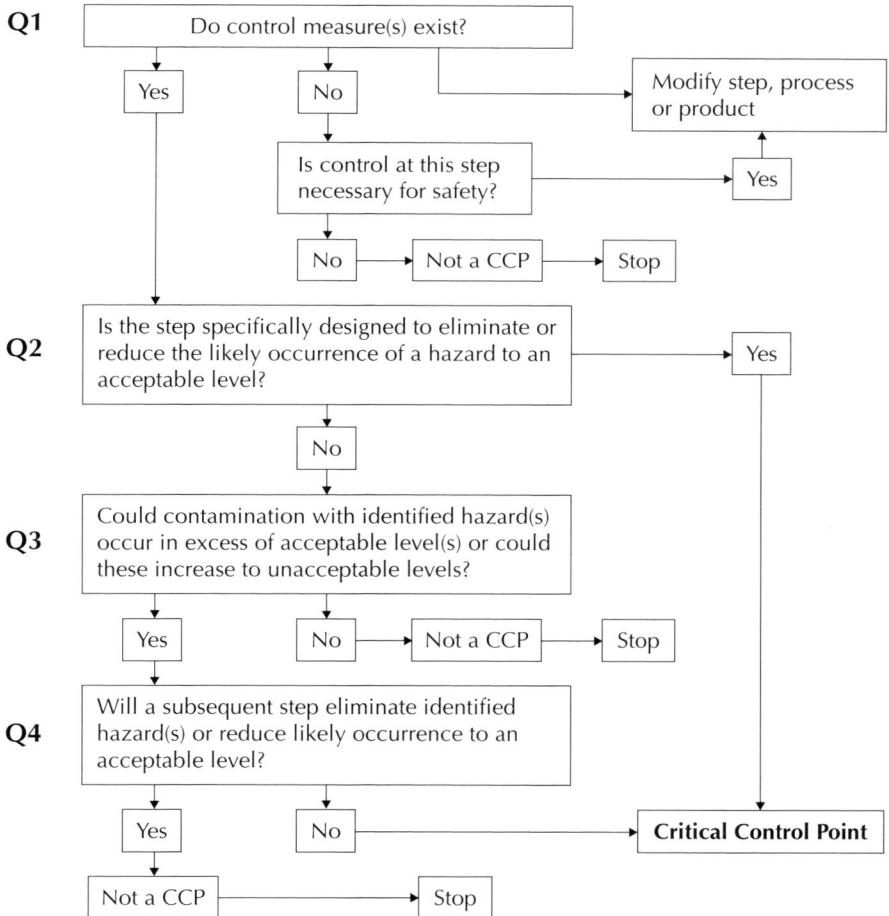

Source: Food and Agriculture Organization of the United Nations, Codex Alimentarius (2001)

Figure 19 – Example of a decision tree to identify CCPs

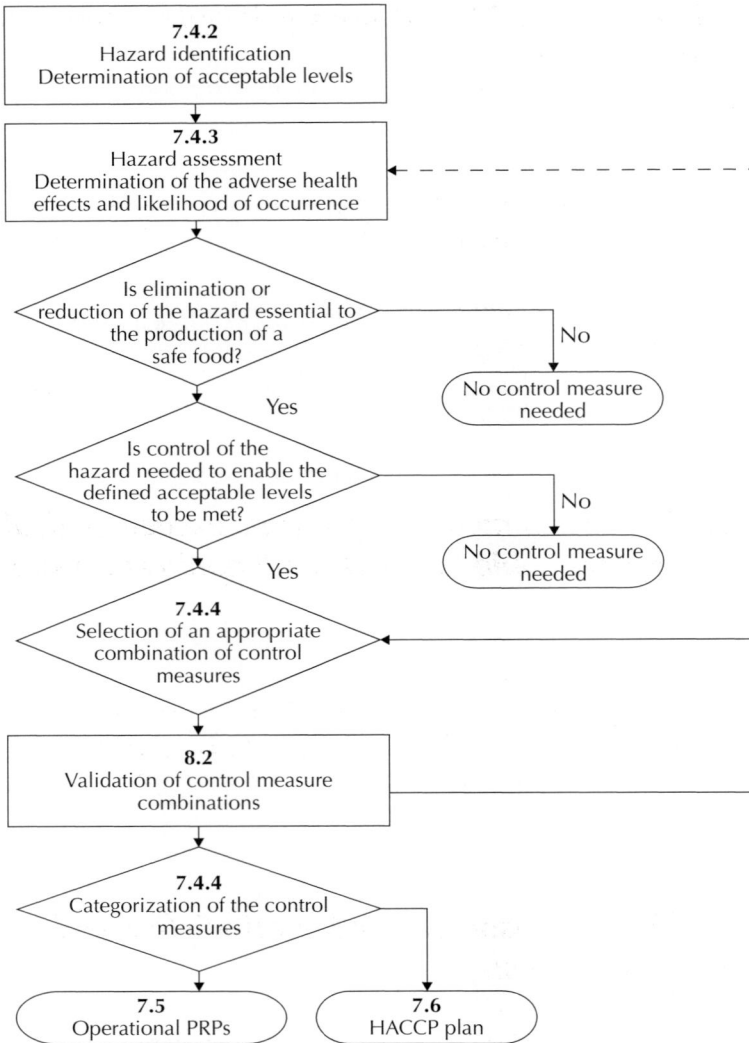

Figure 20 – Decision tree for identifying CCPs

The flowchart shows:

7.4.2
Hazard identification
Determination of acceptable levels

↓

7.4.3
Hazard assessment
Determination of the adverse health
effects and likelihood of occurrence

↓

Is elimination or
reduction of the hazard essential to
the production of a
safe food?

→ No → No control measure needed

↓ Yes

Is control of the
hazard needed to enable the
defined acceptable levels
to be met?

→ No → No control measure needed

↓ Yes

7.4.4
Selection of an appropriate
combination of control
measures

↓

8.2
Validation of control measure
combinations

↓

7.4.4
Categorization of the control
measures

↓

7.5
Operational PRPs

7.6
HACCP plan

NOTE   Cross-references refer to ISO 22000:2005.

Source: ISO/TS 22004:2005, Figure 3

Figure 20 – Decision tree for identifying CCPs

6.4.4 Monitoring of CCPs (Codex principle 4 and HACCP application step 9)

ISO 22000 states:

> A monitoring system shall be established for each CCP to demonstrate that the CCP is in control…shall include all scheduled measurements or observations relative to the critical limit(s).
>
> The monitoring system shall consist of relevant procedures… [including] monitoring devices… and frequency…
>
> *(Clause 7.6.4)*

6.4.5 Actions when monitoring results exceed critical limits (Codex principle 5 and HACCP application step 10)

ISO 22000 states:

> Planned corrections and corrective actions to be taken when critical limits are exceeded shall be specified in the HACCP plan…
>
> *(Clause 7.6.5).*

6.4.6 Verification planning (Codex principle 6 and HACCP application step 11)

When developing the HACCP plan or prerequisite and operational prerequisite programmes, ISO 22000 requires that consideration should be given to developing the plan for verifying that the elements of the HACCP plan, the prerequisite programmes and operational prerequisite programme have been implemented and are effective.

Verification planning shall define the purpose, methods, frequencies and responsibilities for the verification activities. The verification activities shall confirm that

a) *the PRP(s) are implemented...,*
b) *input to the hazard analysis... is continually updated,*
c) *the operational PRP(s)... and the elements within the HACCP plan are implemented and effective,*
d) *hazard levels are within identified acceptable levels..., and*
e) *other procedures required by the organization are implemented and effective.*

(Clause 7.8)

6.4.6.1 Establishing the HACCP plan

An HACCP plan can be defined as:

a document prepared in accordance with the principles of HACCP to ensure control of hazards which are significant for food safety in the segment of the food chain under consideration
(Source: Codex Alimentarius, Recommended International Code of Practice – General Principles of Food Hygiene)

The HACCP plan is a document prepared from the results of the hazard analysis and tends to include the following information:

– the process step;
– hazards to be controlled;
– the control measures to be used (CCPs and critical limits);
– monitoring of whether the CCP is under control (what, how and frequency);
– the corrections and corrective actions to be taken should critical limits be exceeded;

- responsibilities for monitoring, implementing corrections and corrective actions, verification; and
- verification procedure and frequency.

However there are many variations on this theme in use; from the minimum elements that must be included in an HACCP plan as required by ISO 22000 to inclusion of evidence supporting the HACCP plan, e.g. information collected during the preliminary steps (flow diagrams, product characteristics, food safety team members, record of validation of the HACCP plan).

ISO 22000 specifies that the following should be included in a documented HACCP plan:

> …a)   *food safety hazard(s) to be controlled at the CCP…;*
> b)   *control measure(s)…;*
> c)   *critical limit(s)…;*
> d)   *monitoring procedure(s)…;*
> e)   *corrections and corrective action(s) to be taken if critical limits are exceeded…;*
> f)   *responsibilities and authorities;*
> g)   *record(s) of monitoring.*

(Clause 7.6.1)

You may sometimes see this information summarized in a tabulated HACCP plan. The example in Table 2 may be used as a starting point or worksheet and the information input as the various application steps are completed.

6.4.6.2 Operational prerequisite programmes

In the same way that details are given in respect of the HACCP plan, ISO 22000, Clause 7.5 specifies what information is to be included in a documented operational prerequisite programme, including:

> …a)   *food safety hazard(s) to be controlled by the programme…;*
> b)   *control measure(s)…;*

c) monitoring procedures that demonstrate that the operational PRPs are implemented;
d) corrections and corrective actions to be taken if monitoring shows that the operational PRPs are not in control...;
e) responsibilities and authorities;
f) record(s) of monitoring.

(Clause 7.5)

An example of headings that might be used in the prerequisite programme is given in Table 3.

6.4.6.3 Validation of control measure combinations

The purpose of the validation exercise is to obtain objective evidence that the elements of the HACCP plan will work and be effective when implemented, including that the inputs to the HACCP plan are correct (e.g. food safety hazards identified) and the control measures are adequate for keeping food safety hazards under control as well as enabling identification and segregation of nonconforming product.

ISO 22000 states:

Prior to implementation of control measures to be included in operational PRP(s) and the HACCP plan... the organization shall validate... that

a) *the selected control measures are capable of achieving the intended control of the food safety hazard...*
b) *the control measures are effective and capable of, in combination, ensuring control of the identified food safety hazard(s) to obtain end products that meet the defined acceptable levels...*

(Clause 8.2)

Table 2 – Example HACCP plan

Process step	Hazard whether biological, physical, chemical	Control measure	CCPs	Critical limits	Monitoring procedure	Corrective actions	Responsibilities	Records

Table 3 – Example of the headings used in a tabulated operational prerequisite programme

Food safety hazards	Control measures	Monitoring procedures	Corrections and corrective actions	Responsibilities and authorities	Record of monitoring

ISO/TS 22004 gives guidance on types of validation activities. Examples of these validation activities include: reference to validations carried out by others, to scientific literature, or to historical knowledge, use of a guide approved by competent authorities, and so on.

6.4.7 Documentation requirements and updating of preliminary information and documents specifying the PRPs and the HACCP plan (Codex principle 7 and HACCP application step 12)

ISO 22000 (Clause 4.2) specifies the documentation to be developed, the controls to be implemented and the records to be established and maintained. The standard sets out the minimum documentation required, but provides flexibility for additional documentation to be developed to meet the needs of organizations.

Documentation requirements are specified in Clause 4.2 and are dealt with in Chapter 9.

6.3.11.1 Documentation requirements and updating of preliminary information and documents specifying the PRPs and the HACCP plan

Following the establishment of operational PRPs and the HACCP plan, it will be necessary for the organization to update documents on a regular basis to take account of new products, processes, technology, legislation, and so on. Updating of preliminary information could necessitate updating the HACCP plan and operational prerequisite programmes and may result in the need to revalidate the HACCP plan and operational prerequisite programmes.

The food safety team has the primary responsibility for this updating process and for ensuring that the results of any updating is reviewed at the management review stage. ISO 22000 requires that updating includes the following:

> ... a) product characteristics...;
> b) intended use...;
> c) flow diagrams...;
> d) process steps...;
> e) control measures...
>
> *(Clause 7.7)*

In the light of the updating of preliminary information it may well be necessary to also update the HACCP plan and PRPs to ensure that they remain current and valid. In addition changes to the plans will require revalidation and communication of the changes to the relevant and responsible personnel for monitoring control measures, corrections and corrective actions.

7

Creating a climate for an effective FSMS

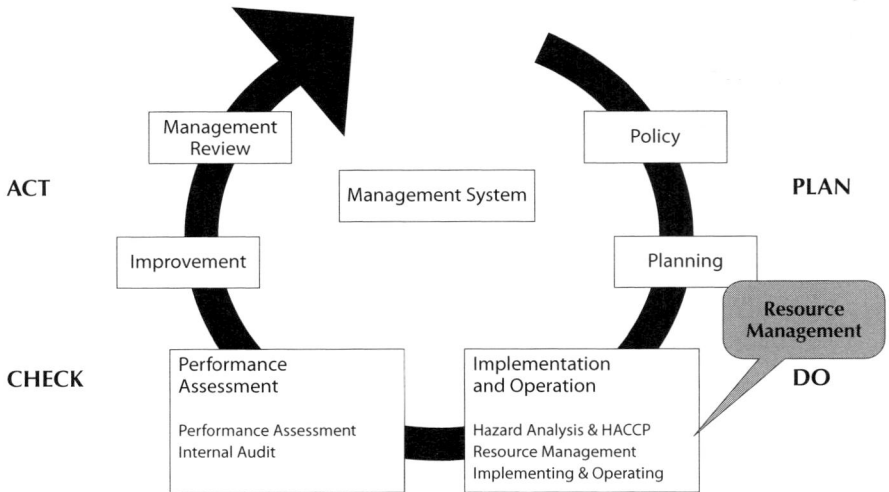

Figure 21 – Resource management

Some organizations appear to have effective systems on paper (or electronically) that are most comprehensive, yet in reality there is little commitment to deliver and the output, in performance terms, is poor.

To achieve a positive culture sustaining a robust system that continually improves, can be difficult to achieve. It often takes time to build up the trust of the workforce. It is hard to ensure that supervisors/managers do not just subscribe to good practices when it is convenient and then forget everything when they have to meet challenging production targets. In the food industry there is often a high level of staff turnover (seasonality of food production being one of the key challenges) which makes the problem of establishing a positive culture more difficult.

The culture in any one discipline is usually inseparable from an organization's overall culture and can rarely be managed in isolation. Therefore many of the characteristics are common. The culture of the organization is very much influenced by the leadership. All too often we see that workers have to wear protective equipment but it seems to be thought unnecessary for the manager to wear such equipment while on the shopfloor. This is unacceptable and there are many such barriers that prevent a positive culture being developed. The following characteristics will apply:

- Staff are committed to the aims of their organization, and the way the organization is managed.
- Top management and senior staff demonstrate visible food safety commitment through the allocation of adequate resources, as well as through their personal behaviour, showing leadership by example. They make it clear that they are keen to hear the bad news as well as good news and they will take action on the information they receive.
- Senior staff and supervisors spend time discussing and promoting food safety in the work environment; commend safe food management practices and express concern if food safety procedures are not being followed.
- Food safety is managed with the same determination as other key business objectives.
- Food safety is a normal topic of day-to-day discussion in the workplace and there is active feedback on performance.

Equally there are many factors that can impair the culture, including:

- inconsistencies in rules and procedures, e.g. types of control measures or corrective action to be taken;
- supervisors and managers not acting upon non-compliances with food safety rules, e.g. when there is a production emergency or there is an urgent need for product to be dispatched;
- controls and procedures developed without due consideration for their practicability, e.g. control measures not adequately validated;
- controls and safeguards imposed by external agencies and consultants that do not take into account their practicality, e.g. generic HACCP plans developed by external agencies or generic HACCP models adopted internally without determining suitability and therefore appropriate application;
- failures to communicate shortcomings in food safety arrangements, e.g. the potential risks to food safety if there is inadequate application of control measures and any corrective actions;
- suggestions for improvements or changes from employees are not welcome and/or are not acted upon;
- there is no employee involvement in, for instance, developing operating procedures, e.g. in the development, implementation and monitoring of control measures;
- there is an acceptance that violations are inevitable, and that little can be done to eliminate them;
- a culture of blame exists;
- underestimation of the magnitude of risk for any reason; and
- lack of support for personal problems, leading to impairment of an individual's ability to perform effectively.

There is no quick way to overcome lack of commitment. This has to be achieved by promoting good practices such as those given in the initial list above. It is essential to involve the workforce and ask its members what needs to be done.

Di Longcroft's Residential Conference Centre, Holbeton
Di Longcroft had long recognized that an organization functions at its best when there was a positive culture in place. She recognized that it took a long time to build up, and yet it could be easily destroyed by one senseless act. In selecting her key appointments she had each prospective employee assessed by psychometric testing and assessed them herself to establish whether they were 'team players' and could demonstrate true leadership.

With a significant number of employees applying for jobs who came from other countries, the need for bonding was an essential element that needed to be addressed quickly. Using her personal experience she developed training and bonding sessions for the teams to ensure some positive culture was in place as quickly as possible.

8

Implementing and operating

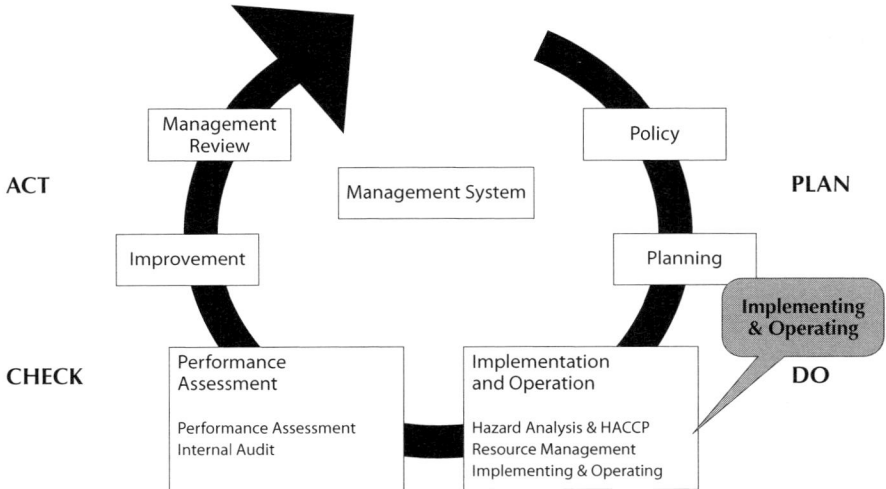

Figure 22 – Implementing and operating

This chapter deals with operational control, management of infrastructure and human resources, documentation issues and consultation and communication. It relates specifically to the following clauses from ISO 22000:2005:

- Operational control   7.1, 7.2, 7.4.4, 7.5
- Management of resources   5.1, 5.4, 6.1, 6.2, 6.3, 6.4
- Documentation   4.2
- Communication   5.6

8.1 Operational control

The planning phase has identified all the areas where controls are required to ensure that the food products are managed safely. This stage of the process is implementing the controls necessary to deliver what has been stated in the policy and objectives. The standard specifically states:

> ...*The organization shall*
>
> a)   *ensure that food safety hazards that may be reasonably expected to occur in relation to products within the scope of the system are...controlled in such a manner that the products of the organization do not, directly or indirectly, harm the consumer...*
>
> *(Clause 4.1)*

> *The organization shall plan and develop the processes needed for the realization of safe products.*
> *The organization shall implement, operate and ensure the effectiveness of the planned activities...Includes PRP(s) as well as operational PRP(s) and/or the HACCP plan.*
>
> *(Clause 7.1)*

> *The organization shall establish, implement and maintain PRP(s)...*
>
> *(Clause 7.2.1)*

...an appropriate combination of control measures shall be selected ...capable of preventing, eliminating or reducing...food safety hazards to defined acceptable levels...

The control measures selected shall be categorized...operational PRP(s) or by the HACCP plan...

(Clause 7.4.4)

The operational PRPs...shall include the following information for each programme:

a) *food safety hazard(s) to be controlled by the programme...;*
b) *control measure(s)...;*
c) *monitoring procedures that demonstrate that the operational PRPs are implemented;*
d) *corrections and corrective actions to be taken if monitoring shows that the operational PRPs are not in control...;*
e) *responsibilities and authorities;*
f) *record(s) of monitoring.*

(Clause 7.5)

The HACCP plan...shall include the following information for each identified critical control point...:

a) *food safety hazard(s) to be controlled at the CCP...;*
b) *control measure(s)...;*
c) *critical limit(s)...;*
d) *monitoring procedure(s)...;*
e) *corrections and corrective action(s) to be taken if critical limits are exceeded...;*
f) *responsibilities and authorities;*
g) *record(s) of monitoring.*

(Clause 7.6.1)

To ensure effective operational control two issues need to be addressed: responsibility (discussed above) and integration.

Food safety activity, in its broadest sense, needs to be fully embraced both within and between functions (e.g. quality assurance, engineering, maintenance, cleaning, production) to encourage close cooperation and collaboration between all parts of the organization.

Often the food safety arrangements for 'support' activities like maintenance staff, cleaners, pest control contractors, and so on are inadequate or overlooked.

Encouraging cooperation can be achieved in a number of ways, including:

a) food safety project teams/task groups comprising representatives from and working with different parts of the organization, e.g. the food safety team leader and food safety team;
b) managers, food safety specialists, representatives and committees addressing problems common to different parts of the organization; and
c) food safety audits and reviews – examining findings and investigating recommendations and remedial actions – can be coordinated in an effective manner.

8.2 Management of resources

> The organization shall provide adequate resources for the establishment, implementation, maintenance and updating of the food safety management system.
>
> *(Clause 6.1)*

This will include:

– human resources that are trained so that they can carry out their food safety responsibilities effectively (Clause 6.2);
– infrastructure, e.g. buildings, equipment, utilities, supporting services and surrounding area (Clause 6.3); and

– work environment, e.g. work space arrangements, protective work wear, availability and location of employee facilities, measures to prevent cross-contamination (Clause 6.4).

8.2.1 Structure and responsibility

> *Top management shall ensure that responsibilities and authorities are defined and communicated within the organization to ensure the effective operation and maintenance of the food safety management system.*
>
> *All personnel shall have responsibility to report problems with the food safety management system to identified person(s). Designated personnel shall have defined responsibility and authority to initiate and record actions.*
>
> *(Clause 5.4)*

The most effective food safety management systems are those where senior management shows its commitment and strives for continual improvement:

> *Top management shall provide evidence of its commitment to the development and implementation of the food safety management system and to continually improving its effectiveness by*
>
> *a)   showing food safety is supported by the business objectives of the organization,*
> *b)   communicating to the organization the importance of meeting the requirements of this International Standard, any statutory and regulatory requirements, as well as customer requirements relating to food safety,*
> *c)   establishing the food safety policy,*
> *d)   conducting management reviews, and*
> *e)   ensuring the availability of resources.*
>
> *(Clause 5.1)*

Top management shall appoint a food safety team leader who, irrespective of other responsibilities, shall have the responsibility and authority

a) *to manage a food safety team... and organize its work,*
b) *to ensure relevant training and education of the food safety team members...,*
c) *to ensure that the food safety management system is established, implemented, maintained and updated, and*
d) *to report to the organization's top management on the effectiveness and suitability of the food safety management system...*

(Clause 5.5)

For effective implementation of a food safety management system, commitment from the highest level in the organization is essential. This commitment is best demonstrated by ensuring that a food safety team leader within the organization has the specific responsibility for ensuring that the food safety management system is operating effectively.

At every level of the organization, people need to be aware of their responsibilities, and to whom they are accountable. They need to recognize the influence that their action or inaction can have on the effectiveness of the food safety management system. Moreover, the responsibility and accountability for the FSMS should be reflected in the management structure.

8.2.2 Defining top management responsibilities

The responsibility of top management should include defining the organization's food safety policy, and ensuring that the food safety management system is implemented. As part of this commitment, a specific management appointee with defined responsibilities and authority for implementing the food safety management system should be designated by top management. (In large or complex organizations there may be more than one designated appointee.)

8.2.3 Defining line management responsibilities

Line management responsibility should include ensuring that food safety is managed within their area of operations. Where prime responsibility for food safety matters rests with line management, the role and responsibilities of any specialist food safety function within the organization should be appropriately defined to avoid ambiguity with respect to responsibilities and authorities. This should include arrangements to resolve any conflict between food safety issues and productivity considerations by escalation to a higher level of management.

8.2.4 Documentation of roles and responsibilities

Food safety responsibilities and authorities should be documented in a form appropriate to the organization. This can take one or more of the following forms, or an alternative of the organization's choosing:

– working procedures and task descriptions;
– job descriptions; and
– induction training package.

8.2.5 Individual responsibilities

To ensure commitment to food safety throughout the organization, the following areas need to be addressed:

1. Responsibilities should be clearly defined. Where job descriptions are used it may be appropriate to include them.
2. Identified individuals should be given the authority and resources (including time) necessary to carry out their responsibilities.
3. Appropriate arrangements should exist to ensure everyone is accountable for discharging their responsibilities.

4. Reporting relationships should be clear and unambiguous.
5. Where personal appraisal systems exist, food safety performance should be included in the appraisal system.

It is important to recognize that organizations are responsible for contractors and visitors who interface with their activities and operations. The food safety arrangements need to take these factors into account. It is not satisfactory, for example, to employ a firm to clean the premises without ensuring that they are aware of your food safety arrangements. You need to ensure that they do not compromise your own products. When interviewing prospective contractors, it is sound practice to find out their attitude to food safety. It is also sound practice to ensure that staff take responsibility for any visitors they receive, ensuring that, where necessary, they are escorted, protected and do not compromise the organization's food safety arrangements.

8.2.6 Training, awareness and competence

The organization shall

a) *identify the necessary competencies for personnel whose activities have an impact on food safety,*

b) *provide training or take other action to ensure personnel have the necessary competencies,*

c) *ensure that personnel responsible for monitoring, corrections and corrective actions of the food safety management system are trained,*

d) *evaluate the implementation and the effectiveness of a), b) and c),*

e) *ensure that the personnel are aware of the relevance and importance of their individual activities in contributing to food safety,*

f) *ensure that the requirement for effective communication… is understood by all personnel whose activities have an impact on food safety, and*

g) maintain appropriate records of training and actions described in b) and c).

(Clause 6.2.2)

To ensure an effective food safety management system, it is essential that everyone is competent to take on the duties assigned to them. It is sometimes forgotten that training is as important for those at the highest level in the organization as it is for those at the operational level. Arrangements need to be made for:

- carrying out a training needs analysis, systematically identifying the competencies required by each member of staff (including senior managers) and the training needed to bridge any gap in knowledge and skills;
- providing any training in a timely and systematic manner;
- assessing individuals to ensure that they have acquired and are maintaining the necessary knowledge and skills;
- maintaining appropriate training/skills records; and
- retraining staff as new technologies evolve.

Remember, those not directly involved in core activities also need to be trained. A classic example is those involved in design and development or procurement of food equipment who need to ensure that the output of their work does not compromise the safety of food to be produced. If food safety hazards are not considered at the development stage or procurement stage, there can be costly and time-consuming delays later in the manufacture and operation stages and in maintaining plant and equipment, potentially introducing contaminants.

It is easy to forget contractors, temporary workers, trainees and visitors. They need to be included in any relevant training programme according to the level of risk they pose to food.

8.2.7 Specialist advice and services

Employers may need to appoint one or more competent persons from within or outside the organization to help in applying the provisions of food safety legislation.

This may be achieved by various means, including the training of staff from within the organization, engaging trained professionals as company employees or by using the services of competent external consultants. Whatever route is chosen, it is essential that adequate information, time, resources and cooperation are available to any specialist adviser. Remember, however, that the employment of a food safety adviser on legislation does not relieve the management of the organization of their legal responsibilities.

8.3 Documentation

This section deals with all aspects of document control, records and documentation. The area of documentation is particularly important in the management of food safety in order to provide full traceability, verification and validation of PRPs and control measures. The whole area of documentation is covered in greater detail in the following chapter.

In brief:

> *The food safety management system documentation shall include*
>
> a) *documented statements of a food safety policy and related objectives...,*
> b) *documented procedures and records required by this International Standard, and*
> c) *documents needed by the organization to ensure the effective development, implementation and updating of the food safety management system.*
>
> *(Clause 4.2.1)*

8.3.1 Document and data control

...A documented procedure shall be established to define the controls needed

a)   *to approve documents for adequacy prior to issue,*
b)   *to review and update documents as necessary, and re-approve documents,*
c)   *to ensure that changes and the current revision status of documents are identified,*
d)   *to ensure that relevant versions of applicable documents are available at points of use,*
e)   *to ensure that documents remain legible and readily identifiable,*
f)   *to ensure that relevant documents of external origin are identified and their distribution controlled, and*
g)   *to prevent the unintended use of obsolete documents, and to ensure that they are suitably identified as such if they are retained for any purpose.*

(Clause 4.2.2)

...A documented procedure shall be established to define the controls needed for the identification, storage, protection, retrieval, retention time and disposition of records.

(Clause 4.2.3)

Emphasis should be on ensuring that the end user has access to documents and is able to understand their content. This demands a level of personal literacy and may even require translation into other languages (e.g. foreign, Braille, provisions for persons with learning difficulties). When translation is necessary, it is essential to ensure that the new document fully interprets the original.

8.3.2 Food safety management system documentation

There is always going to be a need for some documentation (hard copy or computer based) in the food safety management system. This should reflect the particular needs of the organization and should support the food safety management system, not drive it. It should be readily available, simple and understandable.

8.3.3 Document control

Any documentation should be kept up to date and readily accessible to those who are required to use the information. Arrangements need to be made for:

– keeping accessible records of essential documentation;
– ensuring that the responsibility for keeping documents up to date is assigned;
– ensuring that up-to-date information is readily available and communicated to the users; and
– information is understandable (bearing in mind the literacy, understanding capabilities and mother tongue of the intended users).

8.4 Communication

It is important to establish effective communication arrangements throughout the organization if the food safety management system is to function effectively. Equally, it is important to establish communication arrangements with customers, suppliers, trade associations and regulatory bodies, as appropriate. In determining appropriate channels and effective methods for communication, the organization should consider its position in the food chain and the links evident throughout (Figure 23).

Effective communication is a key factor in ensuring a successful food safety management system. Arrangements need to be made for:

– identifying and receiving relevant food safety information from outside the organization, e.g. changes in legislation, information on new developments, codes of hygienic practice;
– ensuring that any pertinent food safety information is communicated to those within the organization who need to know;
– ensuring that relevant information is communicated to people outside the organization who require it; and
– encouraging feedback and suggestions from staff on food safety matters.

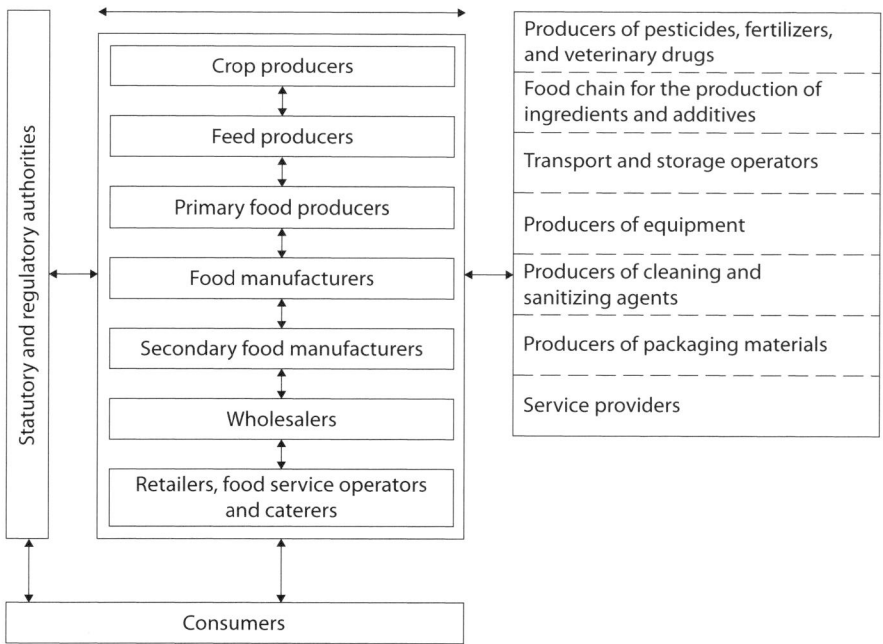

NOTE The figure does not show the type of interactive communications along and across the food chain that by-pass immediate suppliers and customers.

Source: ISO 22000:2005, Figure 1

Figure 23 – Example of communication within the food chain

8.4.1 External communication

In the current climate it is particularly important to be responsive to issues arising that are of concern to the consumer. These need to be addressed quickly in order to ensure that consumers do not respond adversely to the food products supplied by the organization.

Information can arise from many sources including media, customers, suppliers, government agencies, the World Health Organization, and so on. The organization needs to develop its capacity for receiving information and acting upon it and also communicating to external parties.

Arrangements also need to be established to deal with any emergency, such as production loss or product failure. In addition, channels of communication with statutory and regulatory authorities and other organizations should be established as a basis for providing public acceptance of the level of food safety and for ensuring the reliability of the organization. ISO/TS 22004 recommends that, to enhance effectiveness of external communications, consideration should be given to training designated personnel in communication skills.

ISO 22000 specifically requires that:

> ...the organization shall establish, implement and maintain effective arrangements for communicating with
>
> a)   suppliers and contractors,
> b)   customers or consumers, in particular in relation to product information (including instructions regarding intended use, specific storage requirements and, as appropriate, shelf life), enquiries, contracts or order-handling including amendments, and customer feedback including customer complaints,
> c)   statutory and regulatory authorities, and
> d)   other organizations that have an impact on, or will be affected by, the effectiveness or updating of the food safety management system.

Such communication shall provide information on food safety aspects of the organization's products that may be relevant to other organizations in the food chain. This applies especially to known food safety hazards that need to be controlled by other organizations in the food chain. Records of communications shall be maintained...

(Clause 5.6.1)

To meet food safety requirements of statutory and regulatory authorities and customers, the organization will need to establish and maintain the channels by which this type of information is accessed and communicated internally to the relevant personnel to be used for updating of the food safety management system and input into the management review.

8.4.2 Internal communication

The commitment of employees throughout the organization to food safety is essential. They are a valuable source of information in identifying hazards and assessing risk and their cooperation is essential in implementing control measures.

It is not uncommon to find individuals who are well placed to make an important contribution to all aspects of food safety because, for example, of their training in food hygiene or food safety or their past experience. Employees should be encouraged to report shortcomings in the food safety arrangements and be involved, where appropriate, in the development of food safety procedures.

There are a number of ways of involving staff and consulting with them on food safety issues. One very effective method is to set up a food safety committee to act as a vehicle for active participation. Some organizations have found that this can be successfully integrated with other committees dealing with quality, health and safety, production and environmental issues, thus reducing the possibility of one solution causing problems elsewhere. It is all too easy to resolve a production problem and create a new food safety problem, and vice versa.

Information needs to be communicated internally on a range of issues – some of these are detailed in the list below:

... a) *products or new products;*
   b) *raw materials, ingredients and services;*
   c) *production systems and equipment;*
   d) *production premises, location of equipment, surrounding environment;*
   e) *cleaning and sanitation programmes;*
   f) *packaging, storage and distribution systems;*
   g) *personnel qualification levels and/or allocation of responsibilities and authorizations;*
   h) *statutory and regulatory requirements;*
   i) *knowledge regarding food safety hazards and control measures;*
   j) *customer, sector and other requirements that the organization observes;*
   k) *relevant enquiries from external interested parties;*
   l) *complaints indicating food safety hazards associated with the product;*
   m) *other conditions that have an impact on food safety...*

(Clause 5.6.2)

9

Documentation requirements

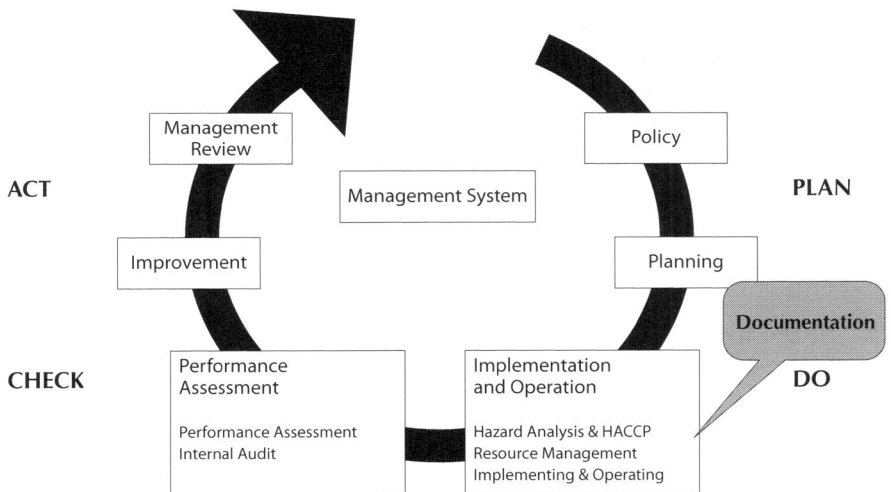

Figure 24 – Documentation

This chapter deals with documentation issues in greater detail than the previous chapter. It relates specifically to the following clause from ISO 22000:2005:

– Documentation requirements   4.2

Although the main clause on documentation is Clause 4.2 of ISO 22000, there are a number of clauses and sub-clauses that deal with documents, documentation and records. These have all been included in this chapter to help the reader identify where there is a need for these areas to be addressed within their FSMS.

Clause 4.2 sets out the requirements for documentation. While there is a need for documentation this should be proportionate to the needs of the organization. The documentation should be present to support the system and not be a tome that is kept in binders on a shelf which is never looked at.

Certain things are required to be documented:

... *a)* *documented statements of a food safety policy and related objectives (see 5.2),*

b) *documented procedures and records required by this International Standard, and*

c) *documents needed by the organization to ensure the effective development, implementation and updating of the food safety management system.*

(Clause 4.2.1)

Checklist 12 will assist in identifying whether all the requirements for documentation specified within ISO 22000:2005 have been completed:

CHECKLIST 12 – Documentation requirements

Clause 4 General requirements

Yes	No	
❏	❏	there is a general requirement to document the food safety management system (Clause 4.1);
❏	❏	processes that are outsourced are documented within the food safety management system (Clauses 4.1 and 5.2);
❏	❏	the food safety policy and associated objectives are fully documented (Clause 4.2.1);
❏	❏	there shall be a documented procedure to define the controls required over all documentation within the food safety management system (Clause 4.2.2);

Yes No

❏ ❏ records shall be established and maintained to provide evidence of conformity to requirements and evidence of the effective operation of the food safety management system. These records shall remain legible, readily identifiable and retrievable (Clause 4.2.3); and

❏ ❏ there shall be a documented procedure to define controls needed for identification, storage, protection, retrieval, retention time and disposition of records (Clause 4.2.3).

Clause 5 Management responsibility

❏ ❏ where external communication to other organizations in the food chain has been undertaken records of this communication shall be maintained (Clause 5.6.1); and

❏ ❏ records of management reviews shall be maintained (Clause 5.8.1).

Clause 6 Resource management

❏ ❏ records of agreements and contracts defining the responsibilities of external experts who have provided assistance in the development, implementation, operation or assessment of the food safety management system shall be available (Clause 6.2.1); and

❏ ❏ records of training shall be maintained (Clause 6.2.2).

Clause 7 Planning and realization of safe products

❏ ❏ records of verification and modifications of PRPs shall be maintained (Clause 7.2.3);

❏ ❏ details of how activities included on PRPs are managed is documented (Clause 7.2.3);

❏ ❏ relevant information needed to conduct hazard analysis shall be documented. Records shall be maintained (Clause 7.3.1);

❏ ❏ records shall be maintained that demonstrate the food safety team has the required knowledge and experience (Clause 7.3.2);

❏ ❏ all raw materials, ingredients and product-contact materials shall be documented (Clause 7.3.3.1);

❏ ❏ characteristics of end products shall be described in documents (Clause 7.3.3.2);

❏ ❏ intended use, reasonably expected handling of the end product and any unintended but reasonably expected mishandling and misuse of the end product shall be documented (Clause 7.3.4);

❏ ❏ after verification, flow diagrams shall be maintained as records (Clause 7.3.5.1);

❏ ❏ all food safety hazards that are reasonably expected to occur shall be recorded (Clause 7.4.2.1);

❏ ❏ the justification for, and the result of the determination (where possible) of the acceptable level of food safety hazard in the end product shall be recorded (7.4.2.3);

❏ ❏ a record of the evaluation of food safety hazards shall be recorded including a description of the methodology used and the results of the hazard assessment (Clause 7.4.3);

❏ ❏ the methodology and parameters used for the categorization of control measures shall be documented (Clause 7.4.4);

❏ ❏ records shall be maintained of the results of assessments (Clause 7.4.4);

Yes	No	
☐	☐	operational PRPs shall be documented and record(s) of monitoring maintained (Clause 7.5);
☐	☐	the HACCP plan shall be documented and records of monitoring maintained (Clause 7.6.1);
☐	☐	the rationale for the determination of critical limits for critical control points shall be documented (Clause 7.6.3);
☐	☐	the system for monitoring CCPs shall include records that cover: measurements or observations that provide results within an adequate time frame; monitoring devices used; applicable calibration methods; monitoring frequency; responsibility and authority related to monitoring and evaluation of results; records requirements and methods (Clause 7.6.4);
☐	☐	procedures for the handling of potentially unsafe products shall be established (Clause 7.6.5);
☐	☐	documentation specifying PRPs and the HACCP plan shall be updated (Clause 7.7);
☐	☐	results of verification planning shall be recorded (Clause 7.8);
☐	☐	records that support the traceability system shall be maintained in accordance with statutory and regulatory requirements and customer requirements (Clause 7.9);
☐	☐	a documented procedure shall be established defining the identification and assessment of end products where CCPs are exceeded. Records of evaluation shall be maintained (Clause 7.10.1);
☐	☐	a documented procedure(s) shall be established that specifies appropriate actions to identify and eliminate the cause of detected nonconformances. Results of corrective actions taken shall be recorded (Clause 7.10.2);
☐	☐	controls and authorization for dealing with potentially unsafe products shall be documented (Clause 7.10.3.1);
☐	☐	a documented procedure shall be established for notification to interested parties, handling of products and the sequence of actions to be taken in the event of a withdrawal of a product. The cause, extent and result of a withdrawal shall be recorded (Clause 7.10.4); and
☐	☐	following verification of a withdrawal programme the effectiveness shall be recorded (Clause 7.10.4).

Clause 8 Validation, verification and improvement of the FSMS

Yes	No	
☐	☐	records of the results of calibration and verification shall be maintained. Where equipment is found to be nonconforming, records of the assessment and resulting actions shall be maintained (Clause 8.3);
☐	☐	a documented procedure shall be established outlining responsibilities and requirements for planning and conducting audits and for reporting results and maintaining records (Clause 8.4.1);
☐	☐	the results of the analysis of verification activities shall be recorded (Clause 8.4.3); and
☐	☐	systems updating activities shall be recorded (Clause 8.5.2).

After consideration of the documentation required by the standard, a review should be undertaken to determine whether additional documentation may be needed to: 'ensure the effective development, implementation and updating of the food safety management system' (Clause 4.2.1c).

Documents need to be controlled so that they are updated, old documents removed and appropriate records kept.

It is quite acceptable for the system to be an electronic one provided the controls specified are met and documents are available where and when required.

The controls shall ensure that all proposed changes are reviewed prior to implementation to determine their effects on food safety and their impact on the food safety management system.

Documented procedures shall be established to define the controls needed (see Checklist 13).

CHECKLIST 13 – Document control

		Have you set up a system to:
Yes	**No**	
❏	❏	approve documents for adequacy prior to issue?
❏	❏	review and update documents as necessary, and re-approve documents?
❏	❏	ensure that changes and the current revision status of documents are identified?
❏	❏	ensure that relevant versions of applicable documents are available at points of use?
❏	❏	ensure that documents remain legible and readily identifiable?
❏	❏	ensure that relevant documents of external origin are identified and their distribution controlled?
❏	❏	prevent the unintended use of obsolete documents?
❏	❏	ensure that they are suitably identified if they are to be retained?

It is essential for traceability reasons and evidence of conformity that records are kept. It is a legal requirement that these records are easily identifiable, retrievable and can be provided on demand to a regulator. They obviously need to be legible.

A documented procedure is required to define the controls needed for the identification, storage, protection, retrieval, retention time and disposition of records.

10

Performance assessment

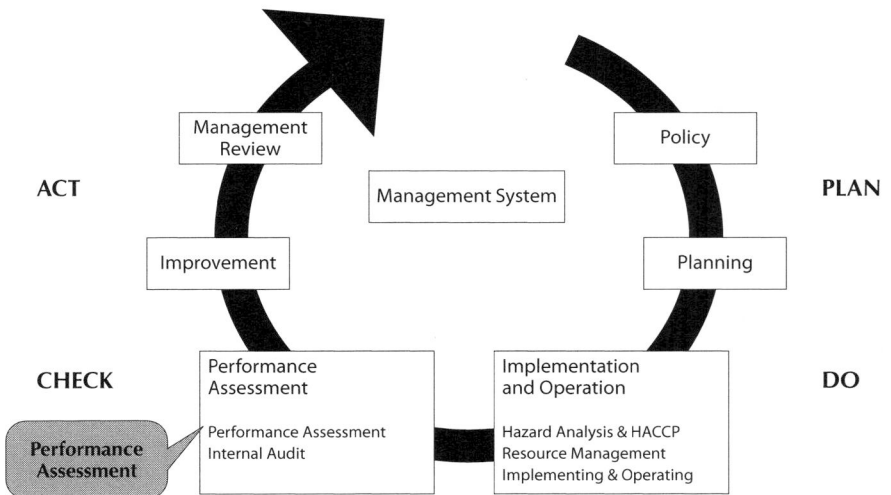

Figure 25 – Performance assessment

This chapter deals with the key areas of performance assessment – validation, monitoring and measurement and verification. It relates specifically to the following clauses from ISO 22000:2005:

- General performance assessment 7.4.4, 7.6.3, 7.6.4, 7.7, 7.8, 8.1
- Validation   8.2
- Monitoring and measurement   8.3
- Verification   8.4 (see Chapter 11)

The fourth area is auditing, a major topic in its own right and which is dealt with in Chapter 11.

10.1 Verification vs. validation

Application of the step of 'verification' in Codex is defined as being made up of two activities: validation and verification.

ISO 22000:2005 categorizes these two activities as separate and distinct. Validation is defined as '…obtaining evidence that the control measures… managed by the HACCP plan and by the operational PRPs …are capable of being effective' (Clause 3.15), i.e. before implementation of the HACCP plan or PRPs.

Verification is defined as 'confirmation, through the provision of objective evidence, that specified requirements have been fulfilled' (Clause 3.16). As can be seen from the illustration below validation is shown as a separate activity from verification in the process for developing HACCP plans and PRPs.

The food safety team is required to: '…implement the processes needed to validate control measures and/or control measure combinations, and to verify…the food safety management system' (Clause 8.1).

ISO 22000:2005 gives a great deal of information with respect to 'Control of nonconformity' (Clause 7.10). For simplicity the entire clause is provided at the end of this chapter. The standard is very specific with respect to the requirements and no further guidance is considered necessary.

Verification (Clause 8.4.3) is dealt with in detail in Chapter 11.

10.1.1 Validation

The purpose of validation is to ensure that when implemented the control measures selected are indeed the right measures to prevent, reduce or eliminate the food safety hazards identified and that these measures will deliver products that meet the defined acceptable limits. This means that the validation exercise is about obtaining objective evidence that the elements of the HACCP plan and the operational PRPs will work and be effective when implemented, including that the inputs to the HACCP plan and the operational PRPs are technically correct (e.g. food safety hazards identified) and the control measures (CCPs and critical limits) are adequate for keeping food safety hazards under control as well as enabling identification and segregation of nonconforming product (see Checklist 14).

CHECKLIST 14 – Validation exercise

Yes	No	
❑	❑	Have you evaluated all the information that was collected during the preliminary steps (e.g. product characteristics, intended use, process information)?
❑	❑	Are the HACCP plan and the operational PRP complete?
❑	❑	Are all elements of the HACCP plan and operational PRP correct?
❑	❑	Are the control measures to be used technically correct?
❑	❑	Are the control measures capable of keeping food safety hazards under control?
❑	❑	Are the HACCP plan and operational PRP clear and practical and capable of being implemented in your organization (i.e. *will it work?*)

Validation can be conducted internally or external to an organization usually including a number of activities, from referencing already conducted validations from scientific literature or competent authorities to microbiological or chemical testing, to verify that acceptable product is being produced.

ISO 22000 specifically requires:

> *Prior to implementation of control measures to be included in operational PRP(s) and the HACCP plan and after any change therein (see 8.5.2), the organization shall validate (see 3.15) that*

a) the selected control measures are capable of achieving the intended control of the food safety hazard(s) for which they are designated, and

b) the control measures are effective and capable of, in combination, ensuring control of the identified food safety hazard(s) to obtain end products that meet the defined acceptable levels.

If the result of the validation shows that one or both of the above elements cannot be confirmed, the control measure and/or combinations thereof shall be modified and re-assessed (see 7.4.4).

Modifications may include changes in control measures (i.e. process parameters, rigorousness and/or their combination) and/or change(s) in the raw materials, manufacturing technologies, end product characteristics, methods of distribution and/or intended use of the end product.

(Clause 8.2)

Checklist 15 sets out examples of validation activities for consideration. This list is reproduced from ISO/TS 22004:2005 Clause 8.2 and tickboxes are provided for you to identify those you have in place or are introducing (1), may apply (2) or are irrelevant (3).

CHECKLIST 15 – Validation activities

1	2	3	
❏	❏	❏	Reference to validation carried out by others, to scientific information, or to historical knowledge
❏	❏	❏	Experimental trials to simulate process conditions
❏	❏	❏	Biological, chemical and physical hazard data collected during normal operating hours
❏	❏	❏	Statistically designed surveys
❏	❏	❏	Mathematical modelling
❏	❏	❏	Use of a guide approved by competent authorities

10.1.2 The need for revalidation

As previously stated, after the operational PRPs and the HACCP plan have been established, it will be necessary for the organization to update documents on a regular basis to take account of new products, processes, technology, legislation, and so on. Updating of preliminary information could necessitate updating the HACCP plan and operational prerequisite programmes and may result in the need to revalidate the HACCP plan and operational prerequisite programmes.

The food safety team has the primary responsibility for this updating process and for ensuring that the results of any updating is reviewed at the management review stage. ISO 22000 requires that updating includes the following:

> ...a)   *product characteristics...;*
> b)   *intended use...;*
> c)   *flow diagrams...;*
> d)   *process steps...;*
> e)   *control measures...*

(Clause 7.7)

There are a number of changes that may require a revalidation of the control measures. Checklist 16 sets out examples of changes for consideration and can be used as a prompt when determining the need for revalidation.

CHECKLIST 16 – Changes for consideration

Yes	No	
❏	❏	New technology or equipment
❏	❏	Changes in control measures
❏	❏	Product changes, e.g. supplier, ingredients, recipe, intended use
❏	❏	Identification of new or emerging hazards or changes in their frequency of occurrence
❏	❏	Unexplained failures in the system occur
❏	❏	Production volume changes

10.2 Monitoring and measurement

Monitoring the system to make sure through ongoing observations or tracking the performance of processes that everything is working as planned is obviously an essential activity, and it is of particular importance that procedures are in place that set out monitoring for each CCP that has been established, including:

- frequency of monitoring;
- who is responsible for monitoring; and
- how monitoring is to take place, e.g. observation, equipment to be used;
- what measurements or observations are to be made;
- what action to take if measurements indicate that the CCP is approaching exceeding critical limits, e.g. process changes;
- what action to take if measurements indicate that the CCP has exceeded critical limits, e.g. what to do with affected product, who to contact within the organization who has authority to handle such a situation in terms of nonconforming product, process changes.

Much of this monitoring will involve measurement of one kind or another, and it is necessary to ensure that the measurements are appropriate and that instruments used are accurate. See Clause 7.6.3.

ISO 22000 states that 'monitoring procedures that demonstrate that the operational PRPs are implemented' (Clause 7.5c) shall be documented and included in the programme information and that 'A monitoring system shall be established for each CCP to demonstrate that the CCP is in control...' (Clause 7.6.4). The systems for monitoring are addressed in Chapter 6 on HACCP.

ISO 22000 states that:

> The organization shall provide evidence that the specified monitoring and measuring methods and equipment are adequate to ensure the performance of the monitoring and measuring procedures.
>
> Where necessary to ensure valid results, the measuring equipment and methods used

a) *shall be calibrated or verified at specified intervals, or prior to use, against measurement standards traceable to international or national measurement standards; where no such standards exist, the basis used for calibration or verification shall be recorded,*

b) *shall be adjusted or re-adjusted as necessary,*

c) *shall be identified to enable the calibration status to be determined,*

d) *shall be safeguarded from adjustments that would invalidate the measurement results, and*

e) *shall be protected from damage and deterioration.*

Records of the results of calibration and verification shall be maintained.

In addition, the organization shall assess the validity of the previous measurement results when the equipment or process is found not to conform to requirements. If the measuring equipment is nonconforming, the organization shall take action appropriate for the equipment and any product affected. Records of such assessment and resulting actions shall be maintained.

When used in the monitoring and measurement of specified requirements, the ability of computer software to satisfy the intended application shall be confirmed. This shall be undertaken prior to initial use and shall be reconfirmed as necessary.

(Clause 8.3)

The monitoring and measuring methods and equipment to be used should be determined by the food safety team when developing the HACCP plan. The purpose of monitoring systems is to give assurance that critical limits for the CCPs are not being exceeded and the process is under control. Monitoring should also enable identification of those situations when CCPs have exceeded critical limits so that any nonconforming product can be quickly identified, separated and evaluated for potential to be unsafe product. The monitoring and measuring methods and equipment should also enable speedy detection of the process going out of control and enable rapid corrective action to be taken to bring the process back under control.

The type of measuring method and equipment used will of course depend on what is being monitored, e.g. time/temperature will require temperature readings to be taken, in line or done manually at specified frequencies, water activity, viscosity, testing (physical, chemical, microbiological, sensory).

10.3 Verification

When developing the HACCP plan or prerequisite and operational prerequisite programmes, ISO 22000 requires that consideration should be given to developing the plan for verifying that the elements of the HACCP plan, the prerequisite programme and operational prerequisite programme have been implemented and are effective.

> *Verification planning shall define the purpose, methods, frequencies and responsibilities for the verification activities. The verification activities shall confirm that*
>
> a) *the PRP(s) are implemented...,*
> b) *input to the hazard analysis...is continually updated,*
> c) *the operational PRP(s)...and the elements within the HACCP plan...are implemented and effective,*
> d) *hazard levels are within identified acceptable levels..., and*
> e) *other procedures required by the organization are implemented and effective...*
>
> *(Clause 7.8)*

Verification includes the internal audit, evaluation and analysis. Internal audit is specifically addressed in Chapter 11. Verification can be considered as periodic and ongoing activities (such as reviews, inspections, certification, testing) conducted in addition to the ongoing monitoring systems developed for the PRP and the HACCP plan, and is intended to provide assurance that the food safety management system is operating as developed and is being updated with the currently available information.

10.3.1 Ongoing verification activities

The schedule for ongoing verification activities should include the frequency of activity, responsibilities for the activity and the procedures or methods that are going to be used. Examples of verification activities include reviewing of monitoring records, training records, customer complaints and observing if control measures are under control.

Checklist 17 provides a guide (though not exhaustive) to some of the ongoing verification activities for consideration. Tickboxes are provided for you to identify those that you already cover (1), those you may wish to consider (2) and those you believe are irrelevant (3).

CHECKLIST 17 – Verification activities

1	2	3	
☐	☐	☐	Auditing implementation of PRPs
☐	☐	☐	Auditing updating of information that inputs into the hazard analysis is taking place
☐	☐	☐	Auditing implementation of the HACCP plan and operational PRP
☐	☐	☐	Auditing hazard levels and whether they are within acceptable levels
☐	☐	☐	Reviewing training records
☐	☐	☐	Reviewing monitoring records
☐	☐	☐	Observing whether control measures are under control
☐	☐	☐	Product testing – end product, in process product
☐	☐	☐	Reviewing customer or consumer complaints
☐	☐	☐	Reviewing traceability implementation
☐	☐	☐	Reviewing deviations from critical limits, their resolution or corrective action and handling of affected product
☐	☐	☐	Calibration of measuring equipment

Periodic verification activity is normally an annual assessment of the food safety management system intended to determine whether the system is operating as planned. This activity covers implementation and effectiveness of the food safety management system and the need to update or improve the system.

ISO 22000 sets out specific areas that must be covered during this assessment:

> The food safety team shall analyse the results of verification activities, including the results of the internal audits... and external audits. The analysis shall be carried out in order
>
> a) to confirm that the overall performance of the system meets the planned arrangements and the food safety management system requirements established by the organization,
> b) to identify the need for updating or improving the food safety management system,
> c) to identify trends which indicate a higher incidence of potentially unsafe products,
> d) to establish information for planning of the internal audit programme concerning the status and importance of areas to be audited, and
> e) to provide evidence that any corrections and corrective actions that have been taken are effective...
>
> *(Clause 8.4.3)*

Consider the task in practice in the example below.

Middle Estate Super Shops (MESS)

MESS has produced a procedure and work instructions for ensuring their chilled food cabinets are maintained at a temperature below 6°C. MESS specified that the temperature on the various units must be checked every two hours using a handheld temperature probe to verify that the temperature control systems were working satisfactorily. The procedure required that an external body calibrated the probe at least once a year.

The internal audit established two non-compliances:

1. The organization was not monitoring the cabinets as per their PRPs every 4 hours at each store. One store was only checking 2–3 times over a 24-hour period.
2. The thermometer had not been sent away for calibration within the last 20 months.

The internal audit team decided that the non-compliances were due to failures to conform to Clause 7.6.4 in the standard.

However, it was decided to establish whether this was the root cause of the failure. It was apparent after investigation that the managers at each location had not been made aware that this was a key area that needed to be addressed. The root cause determined that the failure occurred through poor communication and training.

Following this analysis of the internal audit results, the food safety team decided:

- that the awareness, communication and training on control measures, their monitoring, making corrections and taking corrective action would need to be improved;
- that awareness of the food safety policy and all staff's contribution to meeting it would need to be improved;
- to prepare draft objectives and targets that would enable these improvements to be made; and
- to consult with managers at each location on implementation of improvements.

These decisions were submitted to the next management review meeting for review and approval.

10.3.2 *Control of nonconformity*

All controls should be monitored on a regular basis during daily operations to ensure that the appropriate corrections, corrective actions and handling of any potentially unsafe product are adequately carried out in accordance with defined procedures and by authorized and competent personnel. The key purpose is to prevent unsafe food entering the food chain.

In cases where food has already left site which is later identified as potentially unsafe, then a system for effective withdrawal from the food chain must be in place, to minimize unsafe food reaching the consumer.

The ability to successfully identify and separate nonconforming product will be dependent on the effectiveness of the traceability system in place. You may want to consider testing out how good your traceability system is in enabling identification and separation of nonconforming product on site and when product has left site.

The text given below is from Clause 7.10 of ISO 22000:2005 which specifies the minimum actions that are to be taken for identifying, evaluating and handling of nonconforming products whether on site or when food has already entered the food chain.

7.10.1 *Corrections*
The organization shall ensure that when critical limits for CCP(s) are exceeded (see 7.6.5), or there is a loss of control of operational PRP(s), the products affected are identified and controlled with regard to their use and release.

A documented procedure shall be established and maintained defining

a) *the identification and assessment of affected end products to determine their proper handling (see 7.10.3), and*

b) *a review of the corrections carried out.*

Products manufactured under conditions where critical limits have been exceeded are potentially unsafe products and shall be handled in accordance with 7.10.3. Products manufactured under conditions where operational PRP(s) have not been conformed with shall be evaluated with respect to the cause(s) of the nonconformity and to the consequences thereof in terms of food safety and shall, where necessary, be handled in accordance with 7.10.3. The evaluation shall be recorded.

All corrections shall be approved by the responsible person(s), and shall be recorded together with information on the nature of the nonconformity, its cause(s) and consequence(s), including information needed for traceability purposes related to the nonconforming lots.

7.10.2 *Corrective actions*
Data derived from the monitoring of operational PRPs and CCPs shall be evaluated by designated person(s) with sufficient knowledge (see 6.2) and authority (see 5.4) to initiate corrective actions.

Corrective actions shall be initiated when critical limits are exceeded (see 7.6.5) or when there is a lack of conformity with operational PRP(s).

The organization shall establish and maintain documented procedures that specify appropriate actions to identify and eliminate the cause of detected nonconformities, to prevent recurrence, and to bring the process or system back into control after nonconformity is encountered. These actions include

a)   *reviewing nonconformities (including customer complaints),*
b)   *reviewing trends in monitoring results that may indicate development towards loss of control,*
c)   *determining the cause(s) of nonconformities,*
d)   *evaluating the need for action to ensure that nonconformities do not recur,*
e)   *determining and implementing the actions needed,*
f)   *recording the results of corrective actions taken, and*
g)   *reviewing corrective actions taken to ensure that they are effective.*

Corrective actions shall be recorded.

7.10.3 Handling of potentially unsafe products

7.10.3.1 General

The organization shall handle nonconforming products by taking action(s) to prevent the nonconforming product from entering the food chain unless it is possible to ensure that

a) the food safety hazard(s) of concern has(ve) been reduced to the defined acceptable levels,

b) the food safety hazard(s) of concern will be reduced to identified acceptable levels (see 7.4.2) prior to entering into the food chain, or

c) the product still meets the defined acceptable level(s) of the food safety hazard(s) of concern despite the nonconformity.

All lots of product that may have been affected by a nonconforming situation shall be held under control of the organization until they have been evaluated.

If products that have left the control of the organization are subsequently determined to be unsafe, the organization shall notify relevant interested parties and initiate a withdrawal (see 7.10.4).

NOTE The term "withdrawal" includes recall.

The controls and related responses and authorization for dealing with potentially unsafe products shall be documented.

7.10.3.2 Evaluation for release

Each lot of product affected by the nonconformity shall only be released as safe when any of the following conditions apply:

a) evidence other than the monitoring system demonstrates that the control measures have been effective;

b) evidence shows that the combined effect of the control measures for that particular product complies with the performance intended (i.e. identified acceptable levels as identified in accordance with 7.4.2);

---

c) the results of sampling, analysis and/or other verification activities demonstrate that the affected lot of product complies with the identified acceptable levels for the food safety hazard(s) concerned.

7.10.3.3 *Disposition of nonconforming products*
Following evaluation, if the lot of product is not acceptable for release it shall be handled by one of the following activities:

a) reprocessing or further processing within or outside the organization to ensure that the food safety hazard is eliminated or reduced to acceptable levels;
b) destruction and/or disposal as waste.

7.10.4 *Withdrawals*
To enable and facilitate the complete and timely withdrawal of lots of end products which have been identified as unsafe

a) top management shall appoint personnel having the authority to initiate a withdrawal and personnel responsible for executing the withdrawal, and
b) the organization shall establish and maintain a documented procedure for
  1) notification to relevant interested parties (e.g. statutory and regulatory authorities, customers and/or consumers),
  2) handling of withdrawn products as well as affected lots of the products still in stock, and
  3) the sequence of actions to be taken.

Withdrawn products shall be secured or held under supervision until they are destroyed, used for purposes other than originally intended, determined to be safe for the same (or other) intended use, or reprocessed in a manner to ensure they become safe.

The cause, extent and result of a withdrawal shall be recorded and reported to top management as input to the management review (see 5.8.2).

The organization shall verify and record the effectiveness of the withdrawal programme through the use of appropriate techniques (e.g. mock withdrawal or practice withdrawal).

11

Internal audit

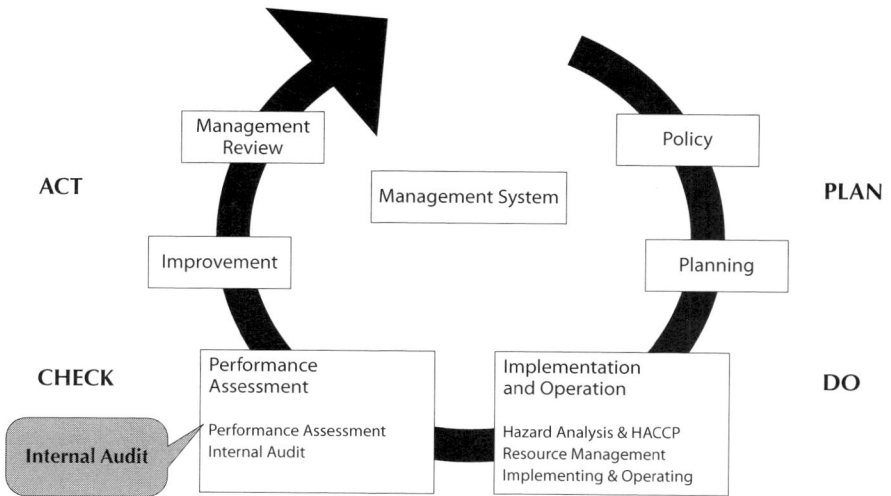

Figure 26 – Internal audit

This chapter deals with the following clauses from ISO 22000:2005:

– Internal audit	8.4.1
– Evaluation of individual verification results	8.4.2
– Analysis of results of verification activities	8.4.3

One of the core management system requirements in all the established management system standards/specifications is the internal audit. A similar requirement exists for those implementing ISO 22000. The audit is the process that tests the system and establishes that it is working effectively and identifies where there may be opportunities for improvement. A system for routinely monitoring performance is insufficient in itself to ensure that the food safety management system is effective and the audit needs to be recognized as an important activity for this purpose. Only in this way will it be possible to judge whether the system is adequate to meet the requirements expressed in the stated policy and objectives of the organization.

Although there is no formal International Standard that gives guidance on how to audit food safety management systems meeting the requirements of ISO 22000, there is a standard that is a useful guide on management system auditing. ISO 19011:2002, *Guidelines for quality and/or environmental management systems auditing* is sufficiently generic to be used for this purpose. It covers the principles of auditing (Clause 4), managing the audit programme (Clause 5), audit activities (Clause 6) and competence and evaluation of auditors (Clause 7) within the document. Those persons within the organization charged with the task of managing audits should refer to this document.

ISO 22000:2005 states the following.

> *The organization shall conduct internal audits at planned intervals to determine whether the food safety management system*
>
> a) *conforms to the planned arrangements, to the food safety management system requirements established by the organization, and to the requirements of this International Standard, and*
> b) *is effectively implemented and updated.*
>
> *An audit programme shall be planned, taking into consideration the importance of the processes and areas to be audited, as well as any updating actions resulting from previous audits (see 8.5.2 and 5.8.2). The audit criteria, scope, frequency and methods shall be defined. Selection of auditors and the conduct of audits shall ensure the*

objectivity and impartiality of the audit process. Auditors shall not audit their own work.

The responsibilities and requirements for planning and conducting audits, and for reporting results and maintaining records, shall be defined in a documented procedure.

The management responsible for the area being audited shall ensure that actions are taken without undue delay to eliminate detected nonconformities and their causes. Follow-up activities shall include the verification of the actions taken and the reporting of the verification results.

(Clause 8.4.1)

To achieve this in practice requires that the operation of the system is checked in all areas and applications by auditors who are not directly involved.

The term 'auditing' is frequently misinterpreted by those who are going to be audited, largely because of the association with financial auditing, which is quite different. It is important that the purpose of auditing is made clear to all who are going to be involved as otherwise there may be resentment at a lot of people, probably comparative strangers, asking questions about how a system is being operated. The object is not to find fault. The purpose is to help, not to criticize. If some area is found where the system is not working properly, the reason has to be established. Is the system itself at fault, making it unworkable in some way? Has the manager or operative not understood what is being asked, possibly through lack of training? The auditor is not a law officer, but, rather, a coach who tries to find out what is wrong in order to put it right.

Although the primary purpose of auditing is to check that the system is being followed and is effective, it is also a primary means of achieving continual improvement of the system, another essential requirement.

If the audit is to be done by employees of the organization (in most cases the best way), they need to be selected with care and given the training that they need. This will consist of training in systems auditing in general and of FSMSs in particular. If there are experienced quality systems auditors within the organization, who are technically competent then they may well be suitable for the task after training on the specialist FSMS aspects. An essential requirement is that whoever is performing the audit does not him/herself have direct responsibility for the function being audited, as otherwise the integrity of the audit may be compromised.

All parts of the system need to be audited regularly – customarily in the course of a year – but not all parts of the system need to be audited at the same time nor at the same frequency. Those areas where the risk is greatest should be audited more frequently than those where the risk is less, and the audit programme should recognize this requirement. Those organizations where the risks are inherently high should audit their systems more frequently than the annual cycle that is appropriate to other organizations. In areas where the system has been changed, it is advisable to arrange an audit soon after the changes have been fully implemented so that any problems arising can be identified and solved.

The results of audits should be communicated to all relevant personnel immediately on completion of the audit so that any necessary corrective action can be taken and improvements made. These results will be an important input to the annual management review. If the auditor finds some serious problem in the course of the audit, this should immediately be raised with the appropriate manager without waiting for the formal report.

Checklist 18 identifies the key issues in auditing the FSMS. Tick boxes are provided for you to identify those issues you already address (1) and those that you need to consider (2).

CHECKLIST 18 – Auditing in your organization

1	2	
❏	❏	Regular, periodic audits of the FSMS are taking place
❏	❏	Staff conducting audits are competent to perform this task
❏	❏	Staff conducting audits are independent from the activity being audited
❏	❏	Audits verify that the organization is fulfilling its FSMS obligations
❏	❏	Audits identify strengths and weaknesses in the FSMS system
❏	❏	Audits verify that the organization is achieving its FSMS performance targets
❏	❏	Audit results are communicated to all relevant personnel
❏	❏	Audit results are the basis for corrective action
❏	❏	Audit results are monitored to ensure FSMS improvement, i.e. there are no repetitions of failures revealed by previous reports

Auditing is an essential element of the FSMS. All personnel must appreciate its importance and all managers must be fully committed to it, cooperating in its execution and acting reasonably and promptly on any findings and recommendations. Staff must recognize that it is not a threat but a means of seeing how the system is working and where it needs to be improved. Everyone needs to cooperate fully and be open and honest with the auditor. In summary, the audit must be seen as an integral part of the process of maintaining and improving the FSMS.

The auditors selected should exhibit:

- ethical conduct;
- fair presentation of the facts truthfully and factually; and
- due professional care.

As a first stage, it is important to establish a process for the audit programme in line with that described in ISO 19011 (see Figure 26).

It follows the well-known 'plan, do, check, act' methodology.

11.1 The stages in establishing an audit system

11.1.1 Stage 1 Setting the policy

In developing an audit policy, the issues which need to be considered include:

- the scope, objectives and purpose of auditing;
- the standards, procedures and aids to be used;
- who is to undertake audits (or be part of a team) and the technical competence and training needed;
- the arrangements for managing the audit, including budget provisions;
- formulating the audit programme;
- the format of audit reports and arrangements for responding to them;

- performance standards for planning and implementing the audit programme and arrangements to monitor it; and
- arrangements for the review of the audit policy and its implementation and for revision, as necessary.

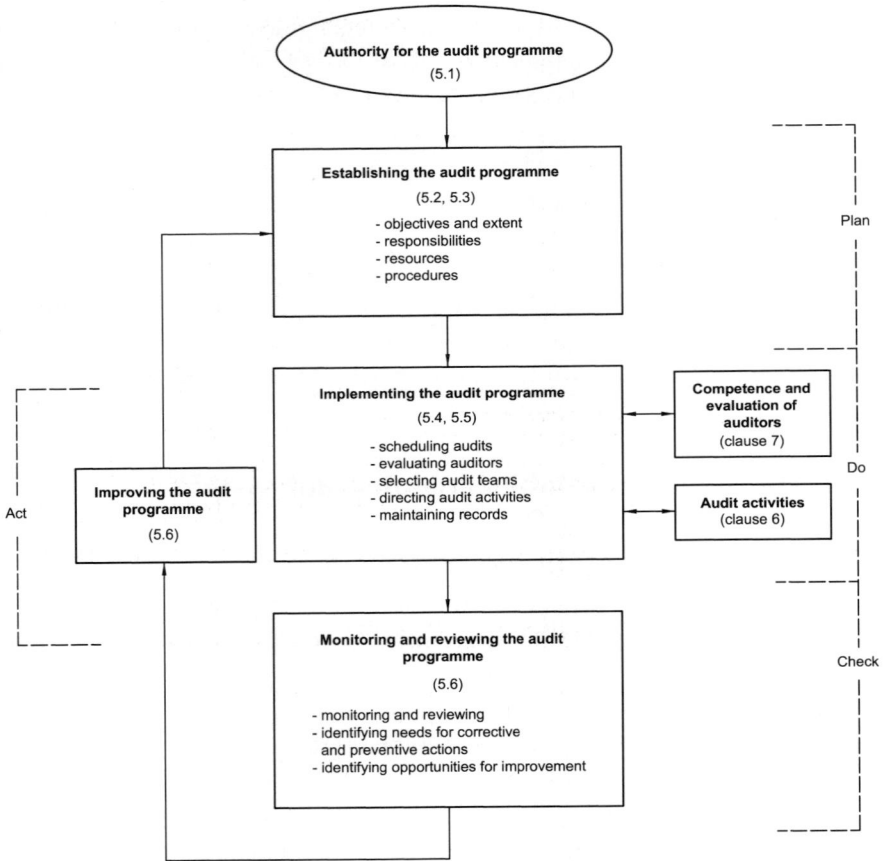

Source: ISO 19011:2002, Figure 1

Figure 27 – Illustration of the process flow for the management of an audit programme

11.1.2 Stage 2 Preparing procedures and aids

Establishing a procedure for the audit will assist in ensuring that the audit is undertaken efficiently and smoothly. Although the staff being audited will recognize its importance, they may easily perceive it as time-consuming and possibly intrusive. It is therefore important that the audit is well organized and focused on the issues in hand. A well-prepared audit will determine the facts quickly and give a productive output that will quickly show the benefits of the system to those involved.

Issues to consider in preparing for the audit are:

- the elements of the audit process, preparation, on-site work and follow-up programme;
- the key elements of the FSMS and any other topics that the audit programme will address and the criteria against which the performance will be judged;
- means of ensuring that the audit includes a representative sample of activities to be included;
- how key questions should be framed; and
- the need for auditing aids, e.g. checklists, aides-memoire, inspection procedures.

The audit system should be based on current best practice and be appropriate to the nature and complexity of the organization.

11.1.3 Stage 3 Planning and managing

Audits cost money. Apart from the direct costs of the auditors (even if they are your own staff who have been seconded to do the audit), all staff and managers will be involved, so there is a significant indirect cost arising from the disruption and distraction from people's normal duties. It is important, therefore, that there is a senior manager in charge who is responsible for planning and managing the audit and control of the agreed financial budget for the audit.

The programme and frequency of audits should be appropriate to the nature of the hazards, the degree of risk, the size of the operation, and so on. As experience is gained, the records of previous audits will show where problems have arisen in the past and where the emphasis should be placed in future audit programmes. Planning should cover:

– preparing the programme;
– the scope of the audit;
– establishing terms of reference;
– establishing a timetable; and
– selecting an appropriate audit team.

11.1.4 Stage 4 Selecting the audit team

It is a requirement of any management system standard that all employees are competent to perform the tasks that they are expected to do. If, as is suggested, the audits are to be carried out by members of staff as a part-time occupation, separate from their principal duties, it is almost certain that they will need training, both in the principles of systems auditing and also in the specific disciplines to be audited, in this case food safety. Even more important is the selection of the right type of person to carry out the audits. If not presented correctly, auditing, as previously stated, can be seen as intrusive as well as disruptive. The auditor must not be seen as an inquisitor who is trying to find faults, but more as a coach or mentor who is trying to see if any problems have arisen so that they can be avoided in future. If the audit is seen by everyone as being helpful and constructive it will be of much greater value to the organization.

The auditor must be able to communicate effectively with others at different levels within the organization. One way is for departmental managers to audit a department other than their own. This may bring added benefits to the organization, as managers appreciate and understand the workings of other departments. If the organization already has staff who are technically competent and who are experienced in auditing the quality system, then they can readily be trained to cover the requirements of the food safety management system.

11.1.5 Stage 5 Collecting data

There are a number of stages involved, including:

- carrying out structured interviews with key personnel throughout the business area to determine that robust procedures are in place and that they are understood and are being followed;
- examining incident reports for the area;
- examining other relevant documentation, including policy statements, risk assessment reports, audit records, manuals, and so on;
- confirming the statements made by observation and examining documents;
- analysing and interpreting the data; and
- maintaining records.

The auditor should always be looking not only for problems (a term to be preferred to non-compliances, as it sounds less judgemental), but should try to establish the root cause of the problem and discuss with the auditee how it could best be overcome. The audit process can be one of the main means of achieving continual improvement, but this depends on the right relationship being established and preserved between the auditor and auditee.

If the auditor meets a situation that requires immediate attention, the departmental manager should be told immediately.

11.1.6 Stage 6 Reporting

For each department or section audited, the auditor should prepare a written report. This should be in standard format and should specify the processes audited, the problems found and details of the actions agreed to overcome them (together with names and dates). The auditor and the person responsible for the activity should sign the report, to indicate mutual agreement on the facts of the situation and any remedial actions.

The report should then be passed to the audit manager or whoever is in charge of the process. The audit manager may accept responsibility for checking that the necessary corrective action has been taken to ensure no recurrence of the problems that have been reported, or this may be left with the individual auditors to clear with the appropriate managers.

More importantly, the audit manager will be able to judge from the reports received on all the departmental audits whether the system is working satisfactorily (there will always be some problems reported, but if these are not many or not serious, the system may be considered to be working), and this will be the basis for the report to top management on the audit as a whole to be considered as part of the management review. This review will consider whether the system is meeting the requirements of the organization, a question that can only be discussed once the audit has established that the system is indeed in full operation.

A more detailed guide to auditing as a means of improving the system, is given in BSI's BIP 2011, *IMS: Continual Improvement through Auditing*.

This is consistent with the information provided above but indicates some of the stages as outlined by clauses in ISO 19011 and is more relevant for those who are conducting third-party audits rather than internal audits.

12

Improvement of the FSMS

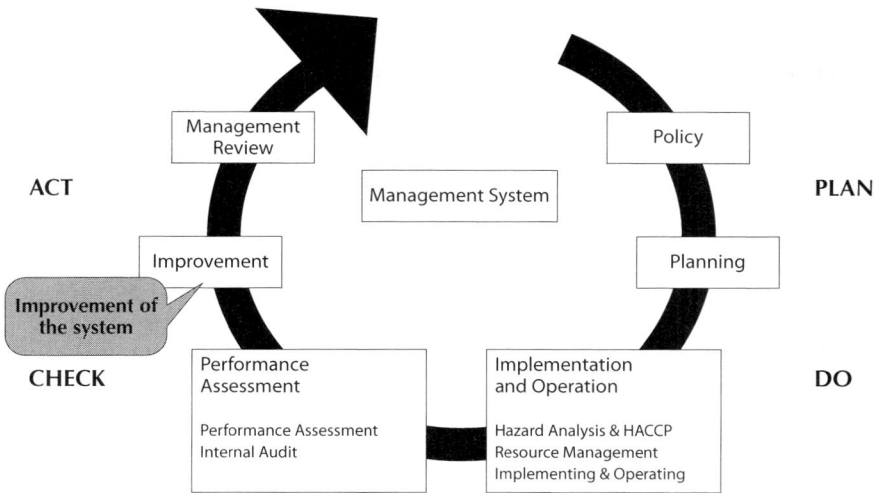

Figure 28 – Improvement of the system

This chapter deals with the following clauses from ISO 22000:2005:

- Management commitment   5.1
- Improvement   8.5

It is essential for any management system to demonstrate real improvement for the benefit of the organization. Systems that seek to implement ISO 22000:2005 are no different in this respect and the standard makes clear reference to responsibilities for improvement:

> *Top management shall provide evidence of its commitment to the development and implementation of the food safety management system and to continually improving its effectiveness...*
>
> *(Clause 5.1).*

Additionally, the food safety team has the responsibility for not only establishing and implementing the food safety management system but also improving the system:

> *The food safety team shall plan and implement the processes needed to validate control measures and/or control measure combinations, and to verify and improve the food safety management system.*
>
> *(Clause 8.1).*

It is important that the FSMS continues to grow and reflect the changes in the organization and its operating environment. The food safety team plays an important role in the improvement process and will be able to draw on a variety of sources from which to analyse potential for improvement. While ISO/TS 22004 does not give guidance on improvement, ISO 22000 does give direction on the key areas to be considered when determining whether the effectiveness of an FSMS is improving. Such areas include:

– communication;
– management review;
– internal audit;
– evaluation of verification results;
– analysis of verification activities;
– validation of control measures;
– corrective actions;

- updating of the FSMS; and
- information arising from day-to-day activities and observations.

A principal source of improvement activity will be in the output from internal audit results. This area is considered in depth in Chapter 11.

If the maximum benefit is to be gained from the continual improvement of the FSMS, it is important that there are effective measures in place to ensure that the system itself is truly comprehensive regarding the organization and also external changes, e.g. legislative matters. However, it is not sufficient for this updating to be undertaken on an ad hoc basis and the system should in itself make provision for this to be planned at regular and appropriate intervals.

> ### Updating the food safety management system
>
> Top management shall ensure that the food safety management system is continually updated.
>
> In order to achieve this, the food safety team shall evaluate the food safety management system at planned intervals. The team shall then consider whether it is necessary to review the hazard analysis…, the established operational PRP(s)… and the HACCP plan…
>
> The evaluation and updating activities shall be based on
>
> a) input from communication, external as well as internal…,
> b) input from other information concerning the suitability, adequacy and effectiveness of the food safety management system,
> c) output from the analysis of results of verification activities…, and
> d) output from management review…
>
> System updating activities shall be recorded and reported, in an appropriate manner, as input to the management review…
>
> *(Clause 8.5.2)*

CHECKLIST 19 – The improvement process (for Di Longcroft's Residential Conference Centre, Holbeton)

Does the organization make use of the following inputs for its improvement process?

Yes No
- ☐ ☐ Communication
- ☐ ☐ Management review
- ☐ ☐ Internal audit
- ☐ ☐ Evaluation of verification results
- ☐ ☐ Analysis of results of verification activities
- ☐ ☐ Validation of control measure combinations
- ☐ ☐ Corrective actions

Does the organization make use of the following outputs in its improvement process?
- ☐ ☐ Internal and external communication
- ☐ ☐ Other information arising from day-to-day activities and observations
- ☐ ☐ Verification activities
- ☐ ☐ Management review

Di Longcroft's Residential Conference Centre, Holbeton

Being a new organization, teething problems were to be expected. All the employees were encouraged to comment. It was emphasized that their comments would be welcome. In fact, Di told all employees that if they felt their points were not being taken seriously, then she would welcome them coming directly to her, so she could evaluate their concern and have an open mind to ways of improving the Centre.

Di was particularly interested in hearing about whether employees had the necessary measuring equipment for monitoring control measures at critical control points and whether the procedure on corrections and corrective actions was being adhered to.

To encourage openness about how the food safety management system was being implemented, Di decided to hold brief weekly meetings that included relevant staff as well as the managers to discuss any problems that had been encountered during the week and to agree how they should be resolved. Di requested that staff involved in receiving raw materials, monitoring of CCPs and filling and emptying the vending machine attend such meetings.

13

Management review

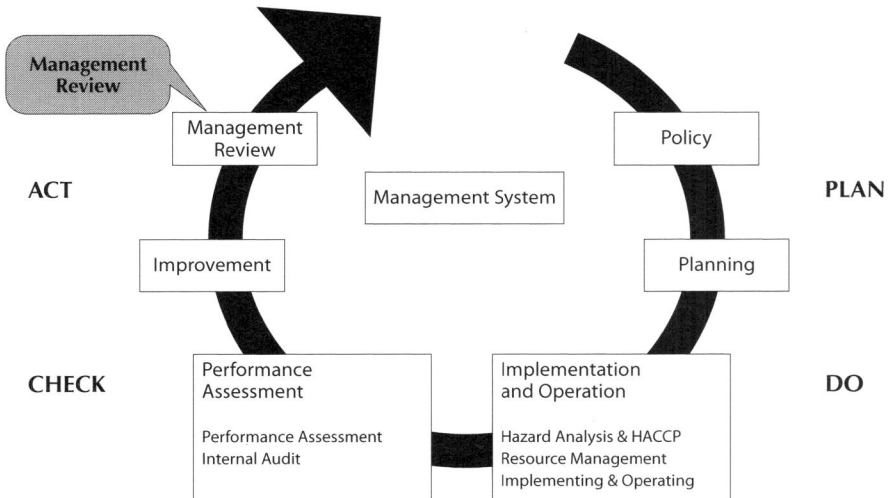

Figure 29 – Management review

This chapter deals with the following clauses from ISO 22000:2005:

–	Management review	5.8
–	Updating the food safety management system	8.5.2

13.1 Key elements

Reviewing management systems is a fundamental requirement in any organization. It ensures that processes and procedures are being applied effectively as intended, and continue to meet the needs of the organization. Most importantly, it provides the mechanism to drive the updating and continual improvement required of any management system.

ISO 22000:2005 states:

> *Top management shall review the organization's food safety management system at planned intervals to ensure its continuing suitability, adequacy and effectiveness. This review shall include assessing opportunities for improvement and the need for change to the food safety management system, including the food safety policy. Records of management reviews shall be maintained...*
>
> *(Clause 5.8.1)*

The standard identifies those issues that should be inputs to the management review and what is expected in the form of outputs. The clarity of the input and output requirements ensures that organizations recognize the importance of the management review and its role in the improvement cycle that is required in implementing an effective food safety management system.

The input to management reviews are required to include:

... *a) follow-up actions from previous management reviews,*
   b) analysis of results of verification activities...,
   c) changing circumstances that can affect food safety...,
   d) emergency situations, accidents... and withdrawals [including recall]...,
   e) reviewing results of system-updating activities...,
   f) review of communication activities, including customer feed-back..., and
   g) external audits or inspections...

(Clause 5.8.2)

It is to be noted that the 'changing circumstances' referred to in c) include both internal and external factors, such as reorganizations, new technology, new projects, new regulations, customer requirements, and so on.

The reviews are expected to include decisions and actions relating to possible changes to:

> ...a) *assurance of food safety...,*
> b) *improvement of the effectiveness of the food safety management system...,*
> c) *resource needs..., and*
> d) *revisions of the organization's food safety policy and related objectives...*
>
> *(Clause 5.8.3)*

A frequent misconception of the management review process is that it is carried out annually. While it should be carried out at least once a year if one is seeking to demonstrate to a certifying body that the ISO 22000 system is operating effectively, in reality the frequency is determined by circumstances. Changing circumstances, incidents, and so on, may necessitate more frequent reviews.

To be truly effective, the management review of the organization's processes should be structured around areas of delivery and involve all parts of the organization. This can involve supervisors periodically reviewing food safety management within a department or over a process, to the senior management team considering the business performance against the organization's targets, objectives and key performance indicators.

The management review differs from the audit in that it is more strategic in its focus. For example, the audit may conclude the system as designed is being followed to meet the food safety policy and objectives, but the management review may show, for example, that internal (e.g. product changes) or external considerations (e.g. future legislation) justify a change to meet the needs of the business. As well as seeking to remedy deficiencies, the management review offers the opportunity for a more proactive approach: to consider where the organization wishes to be in managing food safety issues and how it can maximize the resulting benefits to improve business performance and customer satisfaction.

The organization should define the frequency and scope of periodic reviews of the FSMS according to its needs.

Checklist 20 identifies the key issues in reviewing the FSMS. Tickboxes are provided for you to identify those issues you are already addressing (1) and those you need to consider (2).

CHECKLIST 20 – Reviewing food safety in your organization

1	2	
☐	☐	Top management periodically reviews the FSMS
☐	☐	Business units within the organization undertake reviews of food safety within their sphere of responsibility
☐	☐	Management consider the outputs of any periodic status review to identify opportunities for improvement
☐	☐	The review considers the overall performance of the FSMS
☐	☐	The review considers the adequacy, effectiveness and suitability of the food safety management system
☐	☐	The review considers resources
☐	☐	The review considers the performance against annual and local targets and objectives
☐	☐	The review considers the decisions and actions arising from the previous management review
☐	☐	The review considers the performance of the individual elements of the system
☐	☐	The review considers the findings of the verification programme (internal and external inspections, audits, product testing)
☐	☐	The review considers the effectiveness of emergency practices
☐	☐	The review considers the results of system updating activities
☐	☐	The review considers communications with internal and external parties
☐	☐	The review is forward-looking, adopting a proactive approach towards improving the food safety management system and business performance
☐	☐	New or revised food safety management objectives are assigned either collectively or to individual functions of the organization that ensure a proactive approach to food safety management
☐	☐	The review considers changing circumstances internal and external to the organization that can affect food safety
☐	☐	The review makes decisions on future continual improvement and updating activities

The key to success for each of the case study organizations is how they are managing change relating to food safety as the organizations evolve and meet changing business and statutory demands. In each case, the management review should initiate a proactive response. A significant reactive response is a sign that the FSMS may be failing, although, in practice, most organizations will need to consider both types of response. The first case study is about Humble Meat Pies and the potential food safety impact of an emerging food safety hazard. The second case study is about Waterworks Cakes and the potential food safety implications of increasing production volumes.

Humble Meat Pies

Input

It was realized, following the scare stories about bird (avian) flu in the press, that the chicken used in the pies was imported from a number of countries where avian flu was found to be present in chicken flocks. An emergency management review meeting was convened where serious concerns were raised about the food safety implications following scares of avian flu. It was appreciated that the sourcing of the supply of raw chicken meat needed to be reviewed in case 'bird flu' became a significant reality and impacted upon the safety of their pies.

The ISO 22000, Clause 5.8.2c) and d) requirements 'changing circumstances that can affect food safety…' or 'emergency situations, …' is relevant.

Output

It was decided that due to the serious food safety implications that had suddenly arisen, the emergency preparedness and response procedures would be activated with immediate effect. It was also decided that the following actions should be managed by the purchasing manager and the food safety team leader and the results reported back to top management within 24 hours so that next steps could be determined as a matter of urgency:

- identification of UK statutory and regulatory requirements and guidance available with respect to importation of poultry from avian flu-affected countries from the Food Standards Agency;
- identification of potential new suppliers and determination of whether they meet Humble Meat Pies' specifications and are not restricted by import legislation on avian flu to supply the organization in the UK;
- determination of which of the current suppliers are affected by the import restrictions and suspend supply; and
- contact the local environmental health officer to determine the handling of any poultry in stock that had been sourced from avian flu-affected countries.

The ISO 22000, Clause 5.8.3a) requirement, 'assurance of food safety...,' is relevant.

Waterworks Cakes

Input

This cottage industry has developed a range of cakes which is selling well. As a result, it has identified the need to increase production levels to meet customer demand and therefore is investigating putting on two shifts and employing more staff for the additional shift.

Extra production would entail sourcing of additional raw materials, packaging and distribution capability, extra storage for both raw materials and the finished product, and employing and training more staff. One of the existing final product stores was at the limit of its capacity for storing food safely.

The ISO 22000, Clause 5.8.2c) requirement, 'changing circumstances that can affect food safety...,' is relevant.

Output

It was decided that the following actions should be managed by the general manager, with support from the purchasing manager who was also responsible for sales, and the production manager who was also the FSTL and responsible for recruitment of staff. The intention was to start the second shift within one month. The managers were requested to report back to the general manager on a daily basis on progress being made:

- review the food safety management system and determine its potential suitability and adequacy associated with an additional shift running;
- confirm ability of current suppliers to supply raw materials, packaging and distribution capability at increased volumes required as well as meeting Waterworks Cakes' food safety requirements at increased volumes;
- identify potential new suppliers and assess their ability to meet Waterworks Cakes' requirements on food safety as well as volumes required and cost;
- identify source of additional storage space;
- implement a recruitment drive with the local recruitment agency;
- identify and prepare a hygiene programme for new staff;
- prepare a communication, awareness and training programme on company rules and food safety for all new staff; and
- consult with staff and identify staff that would be prepared to work on the second shift to supervise new staff.

In essence, the management review should consider the overall FSMS against what the organization is aiming to achieve, and decide what further action may be necessary to remedy any shortfalls or move further forward to improve business performance. The main aim should be to identify what future opportunities for improvement there may be, bearing in mind the lifestyle expectation of employees and society, which may directly impinge on the organization.

The management review should be proactive in seeking ways to minimize risks even further, and improve business performance to the advantage of all stakeholders.

The review should not be carried out in isolation from other management discipline review processes as this can be counter-productive. There is little point, for instance, in addressing a food safety management issue if this compromises the occupational health and safety of employees. It should take note of such issues as:

– responses by line supervision to remedy failures to implement workplace precautions and risk control systems which they observe in the course of routine activities;
– responses to remedy specific examples of substandard performance which are identified by both reactive and proactive monitoring; and
– responses to the assessment of plans and objectives either at the individual, department, site, group or organizational level.

The approach should be proactive, wherever possible, reviewing developments within the organization, changes in equipment, working practices, and so on, at the earliest possible stage (preferably at the planning stage), thus avoiding a reactive response to the control of risks when changes are implemented. Deadlines should be set for implementing changes, responsibility clearly assigned and implementation monitored. The new arrangements need to be reviewed after they have been operating for a while, in order to assess their effectiveness and value to the organization.

Checklist 21 provides a guide, though not exhaustive, to some of the sources of information that the management review should consider. Tickboxes are provided for you to identify those that you already cover (1), those you may wish to consider (2) and those you believe are irrelevant (3).

CHECKLIST 21 – Sources of information for consideration in the FSMS

Management review – Inputs

1	2	3	
❑	❑	❑	Amendments/changes to regulations and legislation
❑	❑	❑	Potential impact of emerging legislation, e.g. EC directives
❑	❑	❑	New or revised codes of practice from the Food Standards Agency (FSA)
❑	❑	❑	New or revised guidance from trade associations, e.g. the Food and Drink Federation (FDF), BRC
❑	❑	❑	Present and future types of food safety hazards and control measures
❑	❑	❑	Changes (present and future) to internal organizational structure/staffing levels
❑	❑	❑	Changes (present and future) to the products/services of the organization (including those provided to and by the organization)
❑	❑	❑	Changes (present and future) in equipment, plant, buildings, infrastructure, etc.
❑	❑	❑	Output from previous management review meetings, management meetings or other committees
❑	❑	❑	Information on food safety performance of similar organizations
❑	❑	❑	Staff suggestions and concerns
❑	❑	❑	Competence reports/training needs
❑	❑	❑	Reports from other management key discipline areas such as quality, safety
❑	❑	❑	Statistical trends
❑	❑	❑	Lessons learned
❑	❑	❑	Findings and recommendations as a result of the organization's verification programme (audits, product testing)

Management review – Outputs

❑	❑	❑	Assurance of food safety
❑	❑	❑	Decisions and actions on food safety performance
❑	❑	❑	Decisions, actions and any revisions of the organization's food safety policy
❑	❑	❑	Decisions, actions and any revisions of food safety objectives
❑	❑	❑	Decisions and actions on resource needs
❑	❑	❑	Decisions on improving the effectiveness of the FSMS
❑	❑	❑	Decisions and actions on improving and updating elements of the FSMS

14

Integration

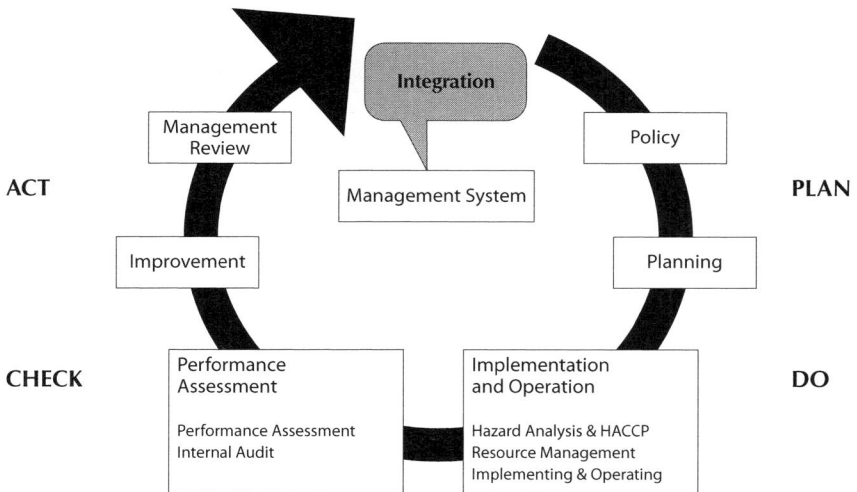

Figure 30 – Integration

Almost all organizations, large or small, have a number of different management systems operating. Many of them will be informal, and may not even be written down. Even the smallest business will have a system for ordering supplies, for paying bills (and wages), for getting the goods to customers and collecting the money. Other management systems, on the other hand, will be more formalized using a structured and systematic approach and be the subject of a management system standard such as the food safety management system standard ISO 22000 that this book is about. Unless you are a very small organization, you will have a system covering the occupational health and safety of your employees and this may well be based on OHSAS 18001. The standard for quality, ISO 9001, is implemented in many thousands of organizations all over the world, with many more following its principles even if they are not formally certified. The environmental management standard ISO 14001 is another that is increasingly being adopted.

Although these management system standards may be very different in their subject matter, their structure is similar in many respects. Each requires, for example, a statement of policy, rules about documentation and records, internal audits, reviews by top management and continual improvement. There is a framework into which these management system standards on quality, health and safety, environment and food safety fit, irrespective of the differences in their subject matter.

In the early days of management system standards, organizations tended to manage them separately. Frequently the quality standard ISO 9001 (or its antecedents) was the first to be adopted. When subsequently an occupational health and safety system, say, was implemented, this was regarded as quite separate from the quality system and the rules about policy, documentation or reviews were repeated all over again. This led to a lot of duplication of time and effort in developing, implementing and maintaining these systems and the inconvenience and expense of separate audits and assessments. Most significantly, there was a failure to recognize that both these systems should be regarded as parts of the overall management system by which the organization was run.

To overcome these problems, the idea of an integrated management system was developed. This recognized that the common elements of the different management systems (such as policy, documentation, audits) could be managed in an integrated way, even though the subject matter of the standards might be widely different. The value of an integrated system is more immediately apparent where two standards cover similar or allied subjects, as do ISO 9001 and ISO 22000. If a business in the food industry has implemented ISO 9001 and then decides to adopt ISO 22000, it would soon recognize that the requirements had much in common and to implement them in separate compartments would be very wasteful and inefficient. While certain aspects of the two standards are quite different, the basic approach and indeed the objectives are the same.

Much has been written about the integration of management system standards over the last few years. Recently a definitive specification has been published – PAS 99, *Specification of common management system requirements as a framework for integration.* This specification has been produced as a framework giving those requirements that are commonly found in ISO and BSI specifications and other consortia specifications such as OHSAS 18001. This framework covers many of the requirements found in all of the specifications, although of course the needs of individual specifications still have to be addressed. The main requirements are categorized into the following subjects:

- policy;
- planning;
- implementation and operation;
- performance assessment;
- improvement; and
- management review.

By configuring the requirements in the specifications in a common manner, it is possible to identify the overlaps and redundancy. This allows the systems to be interfaced or integrated more readily. The approach is shown simplified in Figure 31.

This shows that by configuring your management systems in such a way that they follow the PAS 99 framework, the common requirements can be integrated to the extent that you wish. The specific requirements of the different management system standards such as food safety (ISO 22000), customer focus (ISO 9001) and environmental aspects (ISO 14001) will need to be covered and may need to be dealt with separately depending on the complexity of the organization.

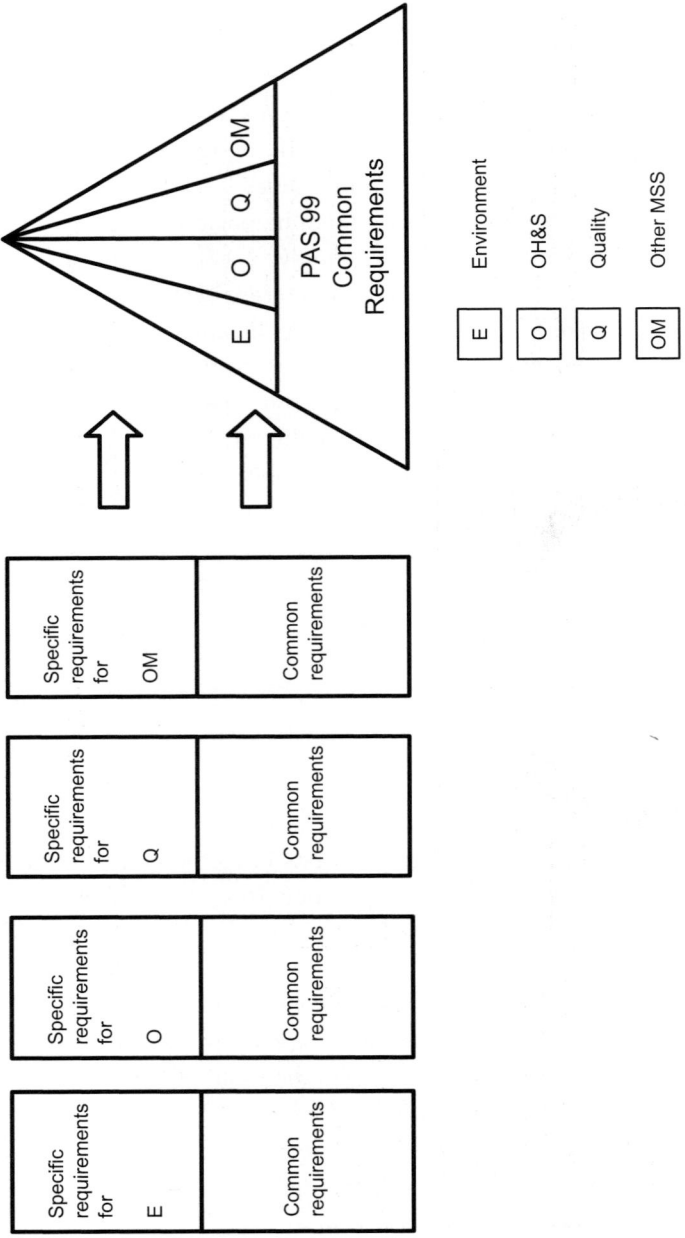

Figure 31 – Illustration of how the common requirements of multiple management system standards/specifications can be integrated into one common system

Source: PAS 99:2006, Figure 1

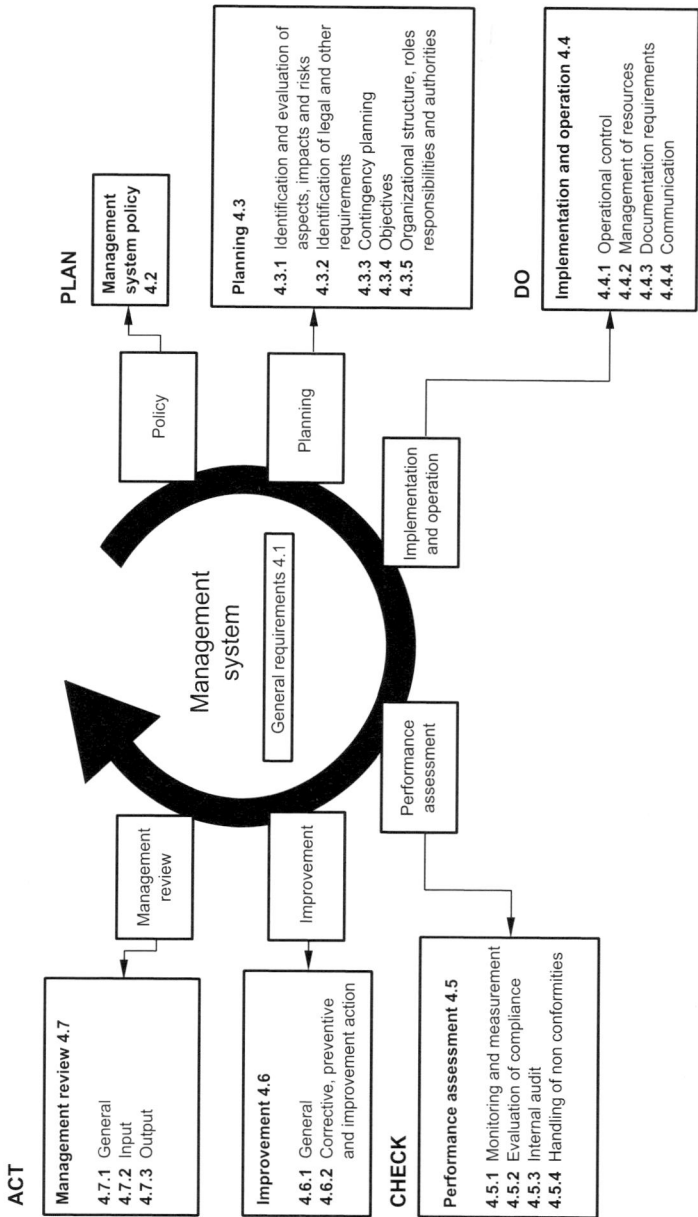

PLAN

Policy

Management system policy 4.2

Planning

Planning 4.3

4.3.1 Identification and evaluation of aspects, impacts and risks
4.3.2 Identification of legal and other requirements
4.3.3 Contingency planning
4.3.4 Objectives
4.3.5 Organizational structure, roles responsibilities and authorities

DO

Implementation and operation

Implementation and operation 4.4

4.4.1 Operational control
4.4.2 Management of resources
4.4.3 Documentation requirements
4.4.4 Communication

Management system

General requirements 4.1

ACT

Management review

Management review 4.7

4.7.1 General
4.7.2 Input
4.7.3 Output

Improvement

Improvement 4.6

4.6.1 General
4.6.2 Corrective, preventive and improvement action

CHECK

Performance assessment

Performance assessment 4.5

4.5.1 Monitoring and measurement
4.5.2 Evaluation of compliance
4.5.3 Internal audit
4.5.4 Handling of non conformities

Source: PAS 99:2006, Figure 2

Figure 32 – Illustration of how PDCA and the common requirements combine to give the outline structure of the management system

Integration **175**

The same framework can be used as a structure for the implementation of an integrated system or business management system. This is illustrated in Figure 32.

Such an approach has been found to provide an effective way to achieve integration and overcomes the sometimes perceived conflict between the 'process approach' of ISO 9001:2000 and ISO 22000:2005 and the 'PDCA approach' of e.g. ISO 14001:2004.

It is suggested that organizations wishing to adopt this approach should use one of their existing systems as a start point. This would normally be the system most established and understood and perhaps already subject to certification. Where ISO 22000:2005 is fully implemented, this would be an obvious basis. This should be reviewed against the table below and any gaps identified and filled. This then becomes the foundation upon which the other management systems are integrated using common processes, documentation, and so on, as appropriate. Table 4 illustrates the correspondence of clauses between PAS 99:2006 and ISO 22000:2005.

This approach is best followed against a structured time frame and set of deliverable targets. Bearing in mind the culture of the organization and its business objectives, it is important to determine the need and level to which integration of management systems is to be achieved.

Table 4 – Comparison of clauses between PAS 99 and ISO 22000

PAS 99 Headings	ISO 22000
4.1 General requirements	4.1
4.2 Management system policy	5.1, 5.2
4.3 Planning	7
4.3.1 Identification and evaluation of aspects, impacts and risks	5.3, 7.1, 7.2, 7.3, 7.4
4.3.2 Identification of legal and other requirements	7.2.3
4.3.3 Contingency planning	5.7, 7.10

PAS 99 Headings	ISO 22000
4.3.4 Objectives	5
4.3.5 Organizational structure, roles, responsibilities and authorities	5
4.4 Implementation and operation	7.5, 7.6
4.4.1 Operational control	7.7, 7.8, 7.9
4.4.2 Management of resources	5.1, 5.3, 5.4, 5.5, 6.1, 6.2
4.4.3 Documentation requirements	4.2
4.4.4 Communication	5.6
4.5 Performance assessment	8
4.5.1 Monitoring and measurement	7.6.4, 7.6.5, 8.3
4.5.2 Evaluation of compliance	8.4.3
4.5.3 Internal audit	8.4.1
4.5.4 Handling non-conformities	7.6.5, 7.10
4.6 Improvement	8.5
4.6.1 General	8.1, 8.5
4.6.2 Corrective and preventive action	7.5, 7.6, 7.10, 8.2
4.7 Management Review	
4.7.1 General	8.5.2, 5.8
4.7.2 Input	5.8.2
4.7.3 Output	5.8.3

Annex 1

Self-assessment of your organization's system for food safety

Self-assessment questionnaire

How to use the questionnaire

What follows is a series of questions covering the various aspects of FSM in your organization. Each of the questions is answered by two statements (1) and (4), which describe two extreme positions. Numbers 2 and 3 should be ticked if your organization occupies the 'middle ground', nearer to 1 or to 4. Tick one number for each question.

In the various chapters in the book there are checklists you may have completed. These checklists will help you to assess your score in this self-assessment section.

Once you have answered each question, add your score to the box on p. 187, total the score, then see how your organization rates, using the performance-rating system on pp. 187–8.

a. Management commitment

Does your organization recognize food safety management as an integral part of business performance by allocating responsibility at the most senior level for ensuring continual improvement in food safety performance?

1. There is no clear management responsibility.
4. We have defined and documented responsibility and authority for food safety management. Ultimate responsibility is allocated to a manager at the most senior level but all managers and staff are actively involved and encouraged in the continual improvement of food safety performance.

a.	1	2	3	4

b. Food safety team leader

Does your organization have a food safety team leader?

1. We have not appointed a food safety team leader.
4. We have appointed a food safety team leader who meets the requirements of ISO 22000 and ensured that their training needs have been fully met. A food safety team has also been appointed.

b.	1	2	3	4

c. Food safety team

Does your organization have a food safety team?

1. We have not appointed a food safety team.
4. We have appointed a food safety team that meets the requirements of ISO 22000 and ensured that their training needs have been fully met to reflect the food safety operations that exist within the organization.

c.	1	2	3	4

d. Identification and definition of processes

Has your organization identified all its processes, mapped and defined them?

1. We have not identified all the processes or mapped and defined them.
4. We have identified all the processes from start to finish. These have been mapped and all the inputs and outputs defined.

d.	1	2	3	4

e. Food safety policy

Does your organization define and document its food safety policy?

1. We do not have a food safety policy.
4. We have a comprehensive and documented policy that clearly defines the organization's commitment to food safety. It is communicated to employees and other relevant, interested parties. It expresses a clear commitment by top management to continual improvement of food safety performance and meets the requirements of Clause 5.2 of ISO 22000.

e.	1	2	3	4

f. Resources

Does your organization provide adequate resources for food safety management?

1. We do not allocate any resources.
4. We allocate resources and make budget provisions to ensure continual improvement in food safety performance.

f.	1	2	3	4

g. Product specifications

Does your organization have a specification for each of its products?

1. We do not have specification for any of our products.
4. We have full specification for all of our products and variants and review them regularly.

g.	1	2	3	4

h. Prerequisite programmes
Does your organization have operational PRPs?

1. We do not have any operational PRPs.
4. We have fully implemented operational PRPs that are routinely monitored and audited at regular intervals.

h.	1	2	3	4

i. Hazard analysis
Has the organization carried out comprehensive hazard analysis?

1. We have not carried out any hazard analysis programme.
4. Our hazard analysis programme is comprehensive and covers all activities in the food processing operations.

i.	1	2	3	4

j. Risk assessment
Does your organization carry out food safety risk assessments?

1. We do not carry out food safety risk assessments.
4. Our food safety management system includes a thorough risk assessment programme covering all activities and processes undertaken by the organization.

j.	1	2	3	4

k. Legal and other requirements
Does your organization identify all legal and other requirements that apply to it?

1. We have little knowledge about legislation that might apply to our activities.
4. We operate procedures and implement controls to ensure regulatory compliance and meet the customer requirements and all voluntary programmes, etc. that the organization subscribes to.

k.	1	2	3	4

l. Best practice

Does your organization identify and embrace any codes of practice and/or other guidance relevant to its activities?

1. We have no knowledge about codes of practice or other guidance that may be relevant to our activities.
4. We have embraced within our procedures what we consider to be the best practice on the basis of relevant industry guidance.

l.	1	2	3	4

m. Objectives

Does your organization set objectives to ensure continual improvement of food safety performance?

1. We never set objectives.
4. We set and publish objectives consistent with our policy to ensure continual improvement of food safety performance, and these are regularly reviewed.

m.	1	2	3	4

n. Employee responsibility

Does the organization assign food safety responsibility to its employees?

1. We do not assign any food safety responsibility to our employees.
4. Every employee is aware of their responsibility for the food safety of those they manage, themselves, others with whom they work and anyone else who visits the site.

n.	1	2	3	4

o. Training
Does your organization carry out training to increase the awareness and knowledge of employees about food safety issues?

1. We do not carry out any food safety training.
4. We have a continual staff training programme to ensure employees are aware of current food safety issues and legal requirements. Staff are competent for the tasks they have to undertake and understand their individual responsibilities.

o.	1	2	3	4

p. Internal communications
Does your organization provide information about food safety matters to employees?

1. We do not provide employees with information on any food safety issue.
4. We have an established communication system to keep employees informed about food safety issues, including policy, objectives, performance, remedial actions and future plans.

p.	1	2	3	4

q. External communications
Does your organization provide information about food safety matters to relevant interested parties, i.e. customers, etc.?

1. We do not disclose information.
4. We have established procedures to inform all relevant interested parties about the organization's food safety-related matters.

q.	1	2	3	4

r. Traceability

Does your organization have a comprehensive documented system for traceability of its products?

1. We don't know what happens to our stuff after we've loaded it on the lorry, and don't care!
4. We have a comprehensive traceability system that embraces incoming supplies, food preparation processes and the output of products.

r.	1	2	3	4

s. Documentation

Does your organization have a documented system for gathering and communicating relevant food safety information?

1. We do not have a system.
4. We maintain a comprehensive system, appropriate to the organization, including a food safety management manual and supporting records.

s.	1	2	3	4

t. Operational control measures and CCPs

Does your organization embrace food safety issues in its operational control system?

1. We focus exclusively on 'business' issues, e.g. products, processes or services, and have no CCPs identified.
4. We have operational control measures in place for all identified hazards with CCPs determined and fully implemented.

t.	1	2	3	4

u. Emergency preparedness and response

Does your organization have a procedure(s) for responding to emergency situations that might endanger food safety?

1. We do not have any procedures for responding to emergency situations.
4. We have an emergency response plan that is tested to adequately respond to food safety incidents and communicate them accordingly. Employees are aware of their role and responsibilities in implementing the plan.

u.	1	2	3	4

v. Internal audits

Does your organization carry out food safety audits?

1. We do not carry out audits.
4. We have a programme of regular audits undertaken by at least one auditor who is both competent and independent. Remedial action is initiated where deficiencies are found.

v.	1	2	3	4

w. Management review

Does your organization carry out management reviews of its food safety activities?

1. We do not carry out management reviews of food safety activities.
4. We undertake comprehensive regular reviews using a designated senior manager to ensure the efficiency and effectiveness of our food safety management system.

w.	1	2	3	4

Assessment of performance

Topic		Score
a.	Management commitment	☐
b.	Food safety team leader	☐
c.	Food safety team	☐
d.	Identification and definition of processes	☐
e.	Food safety policy	☐
f.	Resources	☐
g.	Product specifications	☐
h.	Prerequisite programmes	☐
i.	Hazard analysis	☐
j.	Risk assessment	☐
k.	Legal and other requirements	☐
l.	Best practice	☐
m.	Objectives	☐
n.	Employee responsibility	☐
o.	Training	☐
p.	Internal communications	☐
q.	External communications	☐
r.	Traceability	☐
s.	Documentation	☐
t.	Operational control measures and CCPs	☐
u.	Emergency preparedness and response	☐
v.	Internal audits	☐
w.	Management review	☐

Overall performance

Performance rating
Score

23   Your organization has little commitment at present to FS. You are likely to be in breach of current UK legislation and open to prosecution.

24–69 A level of FS management exists but full commitment by the organization is not evident.

70–92 Provided you do not score fewer than 3 marks in any area, your organization has a comprehensive FS management system in place. This should not invite complacency, and continuous management and development of the system should always be the number one aim of your organization.

In order to assess performance at the start of an implementation programme and as you progress, blank assessment charts are provided below.

Day 1

4																							
3																							
2																							
I																							
	a	b	c	d	e	f	g	h	i	j	k	l	m	n	o	p	q	r	s	t	u	v	w

Day X

4																							
3																							
2																							
I																							
	a	b	c	d	e	f	g	h	i	j	k	l	m	n	o	p	q	r	s	t	u	v	w

Annex 2

FSM Regulations

The checklists in this annex are provided as a guide for further information on regulations, directives and amendments that may be useful to you. Changes are occurring all the time and it is an essential part of your system that you have arrangements in place for identifying changes.

There are many references to food safety in legislation, codes of practice, guides or standards. This annex comprises a selected list of these references which is not exhaustive, and new regulations, codes of practice, guides and standards are appearing all the time. These documents can be downloaded or accessed via links from the European Union's Europa website http://europa.eu/index_en.htm and the FSA's website http://www.food.gov.uk/

You may find it useful to tick those that are applicable to your organization (1), those that are not applicable (2) and those that may apply (3).

Checklist – EU regulations and guidance documents

1	2	3	
❑	❑	❑	Comm (1999) 719 final (Jan. 2000) White Paper on Food Safety
❑	❑	❑	Regulation EC No 178/2002 general principles and requirements of European Food Safety Authority and laying down procedures in matters of food safety
❑	❑	❑	Regulation (EC) 852/2004 on the hygiene of foodstuffs
❑	❑	❑	Regulation (EC) 853/2004 laying down specific hygiene rules for food of animal origin
❑	❑	❑	Regulation (EC) 854/2004 laying down specific rules for the organization of official controls on products of animal origin intended for human consumption
❑	❑	❑	Regulation (EC) 882/2004 on official controls to ensure compliance with food law and animal health

1	2	3	
❑	❑	❑	Regulation (EC) 2073/2005 on microbiological criteria for foodstuffs
❑	❑	❑	Regulation (EC) No. 2074/2005 laying down implementing measures for certain products under Regulation (EC) No. 853/2004 of the European Parliament and of the Council and for the organization of official controls under Regulation (EC) No. 854/2004 of the European Parliament and of the Council and Regulation (EC) No. 882/2004 of the European Parliament and of the Council, derogating from Regulation (EC) No. 852/2004 of the European Parliament and of the Council and amending Regulations (EC) No. 853/2004 and (EC) No. 854/2004
❑	❑	❑	Regulation (EC) No. 2075/2005 laying down specific rules on official controls for Trichinella in meat
❑	❑	❑	Regulation (EC) No. 2076/2005 of 5 December 2005 laying down transitional arrangements for the implementation of Regulations (EC) No. 853/2004 (EC) No. 854/2004 and (EC) No. 882/2004 of the European Parliament and of the Council and amending Regulations (EC) No. 853/2004 and (EC) No. 854/2004
❑	❑	❑	Guidance document on the implementation of Regulation 178/2002
❑	❑	❑	Guidance document on the implementation of Regulation 852/2004
❑	❑	❑	Guidance document on the implementation of Regulation 853/2004
❑	❑	❑	Guidance document on the implementation of the HACCP principles
❑	❑	❑	Regulation (EC) No. 1774/2002 laying down health rules concerning animal by-products not intended for human consumption
❑	❑	❑	Regulation (EC) No. 2160/2003 on the control of salmonella and other specified food-borne zoonotic agents
❑	❑	❑	Regulation (EC) No. 1935/2004 of the European Parliament and of the Council of 27 October 2004 on materials and articles intended to come into contact with food and repealing Directives 80/590/EEC and 89/109/EEC
❑	❑	❑	Regulation (EEC) No. 315/93 laying down Community procedures for contaminants in food
❑	❑	❑	Regulation (EC) No. 466/2001 setting maximum levels for certain contaminants in foodstuffs
❑	❑	❑	Commission Regulation (EC) No. 401/2006 laying down the methods of sampling and analysis for the official control of the levels of mycotoxins in foodstuffs
❑	❑	❑	Regulation (EC) No. 2232/96 laying down a Community procedure for flavouring substances used or intended for use in or on foodstuffs
❑	❑	❑	Regulation (EC) 1829/2003 on genetically modified food and feed
❑	❑	❑	Regulation (EC) No. 1830/2003 concerning the traceability and labelling of genetically modified organisms and the traceability of food and feed products produced from genetically modified organisms and amending Directive 2001/18/EC
❑	❑	❑	Commission Regulation (EC) No. 65/2004 establishing a system for the development and assignment of unique identifiers for genetically modified organisms
❑	❑	❑	Regulation EC 183/2005 laying down requirements for feed hygiene
❑	❑	❑	Regulation EC 1831/2003 on additives for use in animal nutrition
❑	❑	❑	EU Directive No. 2000/13/EC

Checklist – UK acts, regulations and codes of practice

1	2	3	
❏	❏	❏	Food Safety Act 1990
❏	❏	❏	Food Law Guide 2004 (updated by the FSA)
❏	❏	❏	The Bread and Flour Regulations 1996
❏	❏	❏	The Caseins and Caseinates Regulations 1985
❏	❏	❏	The Cocoa and Chocolate Products (England) Regulations 2003
❏	❏	❏	The Coffee Extracts and Chicory Extracts (England) Regulations 2000
❏	❏	❏	The Condensed Milk and Dried Milk Regulations 2003
❏	❏	❏	The Drinking Milk Regulations 1998
❏	❏	❏	The Fish Labelling (England) Regulations 2003
❏	❏	❏	The Fruit Juices and Fruit Nectars Regulations (England) 2003
❏	❏	❏	The Honey (England) Regulations 2003
❏	❏	❏	The Infant Formula and Follow-on Formula Regulations 1995
❏	❏	❏	The Jam and Similar Products (England) Regulations 2003
❏	❏	❏	The Meat Products (England) Regulations 2003
❏	❏	❏	The Natural Mineral Water, Spring Water and Bottled Drinking Water Regulations 1999
❏	❏	❏	Quick-Frozen Foodstuffs Regulations 1990
❏	❏	❏	The Spreadable Fats (Marketing Standards) (England) Regulations 1999
❏	❏	❏	The Specified Sugar Products (England) Regulations 2003
❏	❏	❏	The Processed Cereal-based Foods and Baby Foods for Infants And Young Children Regulations 1997
❏	❏	❏	The Food Supplements (England) Regulations 2003
❏	❏	❏	The Food Labelling Regulations 1996
❏	❏	❏	The Food Additives Labelling Regulations 1992
❏	❏	❏	The Arsenic in Food Regulations 1959
❏	❏	❏	The Contaminants in Food (England) Regulations 2003
❏	❏	❏	The Chloroform in Food Regulations 1980
❏	❏	❏	The Colours in Food Regulations 1995
❏	❏	❏	The Flavourings in Food Regulations 1992
❏	❏	❏	The Materials and Articles in Contact with Food Regulations 1987
❏	❏	❏	The Plastic Materials and Articles in Contact with Food Regulations 1998
❏	❏	❏	The Miscellaneous Food Additives Regulations 1995
❏	❏	❏	The Pesticides (Maximum Residue Levels in Crops, Food and Feeding Stuffs) England and Wales Regulations 1999
❏	❏	❏	The Sweeteners in Food Regulations 1995
❏	❏	❏	The Tin in Food Regulations 1992
❏	❏	❏	The Tryptophan in Food Regulations 1990

1	2	3	
☐	☐	☐	The Egg Products Regulations 1993
☐	☐	☐	The Ungraded Eggs (Hygiene) Regulations 1990
☐	☐	☐	The Poultry Meat (Water Content) Regulations 1984
☐	☐	☐	The TSE (England) Regulations 2002
☐	☐	☐	The Agriculture Act 1970
☐	☐	☐	The Feeding Stuff and Feeding Stuff (Enforcement) (Amendment) (England) Regulations 2001
☐	☐	☐	The Products of Animal Origin (Import and Export) Regulations 1996
☐	☐	☐	The Organic Products (Imports from Third Countries) Regulations 2003
☐	☐	☐	The Imported Food Regulations 1984
☐	☐	☐	The Animals And Animal Products (Examination for Residue and Maximum Residue Limits) (Amendment) Regulations 2001
☐	☐	☐	Agriculture and Horticulture Act 1964
☐	☐	☐	The Food (Control of Irradiation) Regulations 1990
☐	☐	☐	The Novel Foods and Novel Food Ingredients Regulations 1997
☐	☐	☐	The Genetically Modified Organisms (Contained Use) Regulations 1992
☐	☐	☐	The Food Safety (Fishery Products and Live Shellfish) (Hygiene) Regulations 1998
☐	☐	☐	The Food Safety (General Food Hygiene) Regulations 1995
☐	☐	☐	The Food Safety (Temperature Control) Regulations 1995
☐	☐	☐	The Ice-Cream (Heat Treatment, etc.) Regulations 1959
☐	☐	☐	The Fresh Meat (Hygiene and Inspection) Regulations 1995
☐	☐	☐	The Animal By-products (Identification) Regulations 1995
☐	☐	☐	The Meat Products (Hygiene) Regulations 1994
☐	☐	☐	The Minced Meat and Meat Preparations (Hygiene) Regulations 1995
☐	☐	☐	The Dairy Products (Hygiene) Regulations 1995
☐	☐	☐	The Organic Products Regulations 2004
☐	☐	☐	Food Hygiene (England) Regulations 2006
☐	☐	☐	Food Hygiene (Scotland) Regulations 2006
☐	☐	☐	Food Hygiene (Wales) Regulations 2006
☐	☐	☐	Food Hygiene (Northern Ireland) Regulations 2006
☐	☐	☐	The Official Feed and Food Controls (England) Regulations 2005
☐	☐	☐	Public Health (Control of Diseases) Act 1984
☐	☐	☐	The Public Health (Infectious Diseases) Regulations 1998
☐	☐	☐	The National Health Service (Food Premises) Regulations 1987
☐	☐	☐	The Genetically Modified and Novel Foods (Labelling) England Regulations 2000
☐	☐	☐	The Food Safety (Sampling and Qualifications) Regulations 1990
☐	☐	☐	The Miscellaneous Food Additives Regulations 1995
☐	☐	☐	The Animal Health Act 1981

1	2	3	
❑	❑	❑	The Agriculture Act 1970
❑	❑	❑	The Feeding Stuffs Regulations 2000
❑	❑	❑	The Animal By-products Order 1999
❑	❑	❑	The General Food Regulations 2004

List of codes of practice providing examples of control measures, including prerequisite programmes and guidance for their selection and use are provided below (from ISO 22000:2005, Annex C). These documents, as well as updates, can be downloaded from the Codex Alimentarius Commission website: http://www.codexalimentarius.net

Codes and guidelines

1	2	3	**General**
❑	❑	❑	CAC/RCP 1-1969 (Rev.4-2003), Recommended International Code of Practice – General Principles of Food Hygiene; incorporates Hazard Analysis and Critical Control Point (HACCP) system and guidelines for its application
❑	❑	❑	Guidelines for the Validation of Food Hygiene Control Measures
❑	❑	❑	CAC/GL 60-2006 Principles for the Application of Traceability/Product Tracing with respect to Food Inspection and Certification
❑	❑	❑	Commodity Specific Codes and Guidelines

			Feed
❑	❑	❑	CAC/RCP 45-1997, Code of Practice for the Reduction of Aflatoxin B1 in Raw Materials and Supplemental Feeding stuffs for Milk-producing Animals
❑	❑	❑	CAC/RCP 54-2004, Code of Practice for Good Animal Feeding

			Foods for special intended uses
❑	❑	❑	CAC/RCP 21-1979, Code of Hygienic Practice for Foods For Infants and Children
❑	❑	❑	CAC/GL 08-1991, Guidelines on Formulated Supplementary Foods for Older Infants and Young Children

			Specifically processed foods
❑	❑	❑	CAC/RCP 8-1976 (Rev. 2-1983), Code of Hygienic Practice for the Processing and Handling of Quick Frozen Foods
❑	❑	❑	CAC/RCP 23-1979 (Rev. 2-1993), Recommended International Code of Hygienic Practice for Low and Acidified Low Acid Canned Foods
❑	❑	❑	CAC/RCP 46-1999, Code of Hygienic Practice for Refrigerated Packaged Foods with Extended Shelf Life

1	2	3	
❏	❏	❏	**Ingredients for foods**
			CAC/RCP 42-1995, Code of Hygienic Practice for Spices and Dried Aromatic Plants

Fruits and vegetables

1	2	3	
❏	❏	❏	CAC/RCP 22-1979, Code of Hygienic Practice for Groundnuts (Peanuts)
❏	❏	❏	CAC/RCP 2-1969, Code of Hygienic Practice for Canned Fruit and Vegetable Products
❏	❏	❏	CAC/RCP 3-1969, Code of Hygienic Practice for Dried Fruit
❏	❏	❏	CAC/RCP 4-1971, Code of Hygienic Practice for Desiccated Coconut
❏	❏	❏	CAC/RCP 5-1971, Code of Hygienic Practice for Dehydrated Fruits and Vegetables, including Edible Fungi
❏	❏	❏	CAC/RCP 6-1972, Code of Hygienic Practice for Tree Nuts
❏	❏	❏	CAC/RCP 53-2003, Code of Hygienic Practice for Fresh Fruits and Vegetables

Meat and meat products

1	2	3	
❏	❏	❏	CAC/RCP 58-2005 Code of Hygienic Practice for Meat
❏	❏	❏	CAC/RCP 30-1983, Code of Hygienic Practice for the Processing of Frog Legs
❏	❏	❏	CAC/GL 52-2003, General Principles of Meat Hygiene

Milk and milk products

1	2	3	
❏	❏	❏	CAC/RCP 57-2004, Code of Hygienic Practice for Milk and Milk Products
❏	❏	❏	Revision of the Guidelines for the Establishment of a Regulatory Programme for the Control of Veterinary Drug Residues in Foods Prevention and Control of Drug Residues in Milk and Milk Products

Egg and egg products

1	2	3	
❏	❏	❏	CAC/RCP 15-1976, Code of Hygienic Practice for Egg Products (amended 1978, 1985)
❏	❏	❏	Revision of the Code of Hygienic Practice for Egg Products

Fish and fishery products

1	2	3	
❏	❏	❏	CAC/RCP 37-1989, Code of Practice for Cephalopods
❏	❏	❏	CAC/RCP 35-1985, Code of Practice for Frozen Battered and/or Breaded Fishery products
❏	❏	❏	CAC/RCP 28-1983, Code of Practice for Crabs
❏	❏	❏	CAC/RCP 24-1979, Code of Practice for Lobsters
❏	❏	❏	CAC/RCP 25-1979, Code of Practice for Smoked Fish
❏	❏	❏	CAC/RCP 26-1979, Code of Practice for Salted Fish
❏	❏	❏	CAC/RCP 17-1978, Code of Practice for Shrimps or Prawns
❏	❏	❏	CAC/RCP 18-1978, Code of Hygienic Practice for Molluscan Shellfish
❏	❏	❏	CAC/RCP 52-2003, Code of Practice for Fish and Fishery Products
❏	❏	❏	C.1.10 CAC/RCP 52-2003 (Rev. 2-2005) Code of Practice for Fish and Fishery Products (aquaculture)

1	2	3	**Waters**
❏	❏	❏	CAC/RCP 33-1985, Code of Hygienic Practice for the Collection, Processing and Marketing of Natural Mineral Waters
❏	❏	❏	CAC/RCP 48-2001, Code of Hygienic Practice for Bottled/Packaged Drinking Waters (Other than Natural Mineral Waters)

Transportation

❏	❏	❏	CAC/RCP 47-2001, Code of Hygienic Practice for the Transport of Food in Bulk and Semi-packed Food
❏	❏	❏	CAC/RCP 36-1987 (Rev. 1-1999), Code of Practice for the Storage and Transport of Edible Oils and Fats in Bulk
❏	❏	❏	CAC/RCP 44-1995, Code of Practice for Packaging and Transport of Tropical Fresh Fruit and Vegetables

Retail

❏	❏	❏	CAC/RCP 43-1997 (Rev. 1-2001), Code of Hygienic Practice for the Preparation and Sale of Street Foods (Regional Code – Latin America and the Caribbean)
❏	❏	❏	CAC/RCP 39-1993, Code of Hygienic Practice for Precooked and Cooked Foods in Mass Catering
❏	❏	❏	CAC/GL 22-1997 (Rev. 1-1999), Guidelines for the Design of Control Measures for Street-vended Foods in Africa

Food safety hazard specific codes and guidelines

❏	❏	❏	CAC/RCP 38-1993, Code of Practice for Control of the Use of Veterinary Drugs
❏	❏	❏	CAC/RCP 50-2003, Code of Practice for the Prevention of Patulin Contamination in Apple Juice and Apple Juice Ingredients in other Beverages
❏	❏	❏	CAC/RCP 51-2003, Code of Practice for the Prevention of Mycotoxin Contamination in Cereals, including Annexes on Ochratoxin A, Zearalenone, Fumonisin and Tricothecenes
❏	❏	❏	CAC/RCP 55-2004, Code of Practice for the Prevention and Reduction of Aflatoxin Contamination in Peanuts
❏	❏	❏	CAC/RCP 56-2004, Code of Practice for the Prevention and Reduction of Lead Contamination in Foods
❏	❏	❏	CAC/RCP 60-2005 Code of Practice for the Prevention and Reduction of Inorganic Tin Contamination in Canned Foods
❏	❏	❏	CAC/RCP 61-2005 Code of Practice to Minimise and Contain Antimicrobial Resistance
❏	❏	❏	CAC/RCP 59-2005 Code of Practice for the Prevention and Reduction of Aflatoxin Contamination in Treenuts
❏	❏	❏	Guidelines for the Control of Listeria monocytogenes in Foods

Control measure-specific codes and guidelines

❏	❏	❏	CAC/RCP 19-1979 (Rev. 1-1983), Code of Practice for the Operation of Irradiation Facilities Used for the Treatment of Foods
❏	❏	❏	CAC/RCP 40-1993, Code of Hygienic Practice for Aseptically Processed and Packaged Low-acid Foods

1	2	3	
❑	❑	❑	CAC/RCP 49-2001, Code of Practice for Source Directed Measures to Reduce Contamination of Food with Chemicals
❑	❑	❑	CAC/GL 13-1991, Guidelines for the Preservation of Raw Milk by Use of the Lactoperoxidase System
❑	❑	❑	CAC/STAN 106-1983 (Rev. 1-2003), General Standard for Irradiated Foods

BSI publications for the food industry

Processes in the food industry

❑	❑	❑	BS ISO 8086:2004, *Dairy plant — Hygiene conditions — General guidance on inspection and sampling procedures*
❑	❑	❑	BIP 2049:2006, *Winning with Food Safety. A Guide for business*
❑	❑	❑	BIP 3006:2004, *Healthy distance food hygiene training*
❑	❑	❑	05/30131998 DC, BS EN 15180, *Food processing machinery — Forming machines — Safety and hygiene requirements*
❑	❑	❑	05/30130669 DC, BS EN 15165, *Food processing machinery — Forming machines — Safety and hygiene requirements*
❑	❑	❑	05/30130673 DC, BS EN 15166, *Food processing machinery — Automatic back splitting machines of butchery carcasses — Safety and hygiene requirements*
❑	❑	❑	BS 7771:1994, *Code of practice for pasteurization of milk on farms and in small dairies*

Food products in general

❑	❑	❑	BS EN 12856:1999, *Foodstuffs — Determination of acesulfame-K, aspartame and saccharin — High performance liquid chromatographic method*
❑	❑	❑	BS EN 12857:1999, *Foodstuffs — Determination of cyclamate — High performance liquid chromatographic method*

General methods of tests and analysis for food products

❑	❑	❑	BS 6215-1:1981, *Methods of test for agricultural food products — Part 1: Determination of crude fibre content (general method)*
❑	❑	❑	BS 6215-2:1981, *Methods of test for agricultural food products — Part 2: Determination of crude fibre content (modified Scharrer method)*
❑	❑	❑	BS EN ISO 21571:2005, *Foodstuffs — Methods of analysis for the detection of genetically modified organisms and derived products. Nucleic acid extraction*
❑	❑	❑	BS EN 1784:2003, *Foodstuffs — Detection of irradiated food containing fat — Gas chromatographic analysis of hydrocarbons*
❑	❑	❑	BS EN 1785:2003, *Foodstuffs — Detection of irradiated food containing fat — Gas chromatographic/mass spectrometric analysis of 2-alkylcyclobutanones*
❑	❑	❑	BS EN 1786:1997, *Foodstuffs — Detection of irradiated food containing bone — Method by ESR spectroscopy*

1	2	3	
❏	❏	❏	BS EN 1787:2000, *Foodstuffs — Detection of irradiated food containing cellulose by ESR spectroscopy*
❏	❏	❏	BS EN 1788:2001, *Foodstuffs — Thermoluminescence detection of irradiated food from which silicate minerals can be isolated*
❏	❏	❏	BS EN 1988-1:1998, *Foodstuffs — Determination of sulfite — Part 1: Optimized Monier-Williams method*
❏	❏	❏	BS EN 1988-2:1998, *Foodstuffs — Determination of sulfite — Part 2: Enzymatic method*
❏	❏	❏	BS EN 12014-1:1997, *Foodstuffs — Determination of nitrate and/or nitrite content — Part 1: General considerations*
❏	❏	❏	BS EN 12393-1:1999, *Non-fatty foods — Multiresidue methods for the gas chromatographic determination of pesticide residues — Part 1: General considerations*
❏	❏	❏	BS EN 12393-2:1999, *Non-fatty foods — Multiresidue methods for the gas chromatographic determination of pesticide residues — Part 2: Methods for extraction and clean-up*
❏	❏	❏	BS EN 12393-3:1999, *Non-fatty foods — Multiresidue methods for the gas chromatographic determination of pesticide residues — Part 3: Determination and confirmatory tests*
❏	❏	❏	BS EN 12396-1:1999, *Non-fatty foods — Determination of dithiocarbamate and thiuram disulfide residues — Part 1: Spectrometric method*
❏	❏	❏	BS EN 12396-2:1999, *Non-fatty foods — Determination of dithiocarbamate and thiuram disulfide residues — Part 2: Gaschromatographic method*
❏	❏	❏	BS EN 12396-3:2000, *Non-fatty foods — Determination of dithiocarbamate and thiuram disulfide residues — Part 3: UV spectrometric xanthogenate method*
❏	❏	❏	BS EN 12821:2000, *Foodstuffs — Determination of vitamin D by high perfomance liquid chromatography — Measurement of cholecalciferol (D3) and ergocalciferol (D2)*
❏	❏	❏	BS EN 12822:2000, *Foodstuffs — Determination of vitamin E by high performance liquid chromatography — Measurement of alpha-, beta-, gamma- and delta-tocopherols*
❏	❏	❏	BS EN 12823-1:2000, *Foodstuffs — Determination of vitamin A by high performance liquid chromatography — Part 1: Measurement of all-trans-retinol and 13-cis-retinol*
❏	❏	❏	BS EN 12823-2:2000, *Foodstuffs — Determination of vitamin A by high performance liquid chromatography — Part 2: Measurement of beta-carotene*
❏	❏	❏	BS EN 13191-1:2000, *Non-fatty food — Determination of bromide residues — Part 1: Determination of total bromide as inorganic bromide*
❏	❏	❏	BS EN 13191-2:2000, *Non-fatty food — Determination of bromide residues — Part 2: Determination of inorganic bromide*
❏	❏	❏	BS EN 13708:2002, *Foodstuffs — Detection of irradiated food containing crystalline sugar by ESR spectroscopy*
❏	❏	❏	BS EN 13751:2002, *Foodstuffs — Detection of irradiated food using photo stimulated luminescence*
❏	❏	❏	BS EN 13783:2002, *Foodstuffs — Detection of irradiated food using Direct Epifluorescent Filter Technique/Aerobic Plate Count (DEFT/APC) — Screening method*
❏	❏	❏	BS EN 13784:2002, *Foodstuffs — DNA comet assay for the detection of irradiated foodstuffs — Screening method*

1	2	3	
❑	❑	❑	BS EN 13804:2002, *Foodstuffs — Determination of trace elements — Performance criteria, general considerations and sample preparation*
❑	❑	❑	BS EN 13805:2002, *Foodstuffs — Determination of trace elements — Pressure digestion*
❑	❑	❑	BS EN 13806:2002, *Foodstuffs — Determination of trace elements — Determination of mercury by cold-vapour atomic absorption spectrometry (CVAAS) after pressure digestion*
❑	❑	❑	BS EN 14082:2003, *Foodstuffs — Determination of trace elements — Determination of lead, cadmium, zinc, copper, iron and chromium by atomic absorption spectrometry (AAS) after ash drying*
❑	❑	❑	BS EN 14083:2003, *Foodstuffs — Determination of trace elements — Determination of lead, cadmium, chromium and molybdenum by graphite furnace atomic absorption spectrometry (GFAAS) after pressure digestion*
❑	❑	❑	BS EN 14084:2003, *Foodstuffs — Determination of trace elements — Determination of lead, cadmium, zinc, copper and iron by atomic absorption spectrometry (AAS) after microwave digestion*
❑	❑	❑	BS EN 14122:2003, *Foodstuffs — Determination of vitamin B1 by HPLC*
❑	❑	❑	BS EN 14123:2003, *Foodstuffs — Determination of aflatoxin B1 and the sum of aflatoxin B_1, B_2, G_1 and G_2 in peanuts, pistachios, figs, and paprika powder — High performance liquid chromatographic method with postcolumn derivatization and immunoaffinity column clean-up*
❑	❑	❑	BS EN 14130:2003, *Foodstuffs — Determination of vitamin C by HPLC*
❑	❑	❑	BS EN 14148:2003, *Foodstuffs — Determination of vitamin K1 by HPLC*
❑	❑	❑	BS EN 14152:2003, *Foodstuffs — Determination of vitamin B2 by HPLC*
❑	❑	❑	DD ENV 14164:2002, *Foodstuffs — Determination of vitamin B6 by HPLC*
❑	❑	❑	DD ENV 14166:2001, *Foodstuffs — Determination of vitamin B6 by microbiological assay*
❑	❑	❑	DD CEN/TS 14537:2003, *Foodstuffs — Determination of neohesperidin-dihydrochalcon*
❑	❑	❑	BS EN 14546:2005, *Foodstuffs — Determination of trace elements — Determination of total arsenic by hydride generation atomic absorption spectrometry (HGAAS) after dry ashing*
❑	❑	❑	BS EN 14573:2004, *Foodstuffs — Determination of 3-monochloropropane-1,2-diol by GC/MS*
❑	❑	❑	BS EN 14627:2005, *Foodstuffs — Determination of trace elements — Determination of total arsenic and selenium by hydride generation atomic absorption spectrometry (HGAAS) after pressure digestion*
❑	❑	❑	DD CEN/TS 15111:2005, *Foodstuffs — Determination of trace elements — Determination of iodine in dietetic foods by ICP-MS (inductively coupled plasma mass spectrometry)*
❑	❑	❑	BS EN ISO 21569:2005, *Foodstuffs — Methods of analysis for the detection of genetically modified organisms and derived products — Qualitative nucleic acid based methods*
❑	❑	❑	BS EN 12955:1999, *Foodstuffs — Determination of aflatoxin B1, and the sum of aflatoxins B_1, G_1 and G_2 in cereals, shell-fruits and derived products — High performance liquid chromatographic method with post column derivatization and immunoaffinity column clean up*
❑	❑	❑	BS EN 13610:2002, *Chemical disinfectants — Quantitative suspension test for the evaluation of virucidal activity against bacteriophages of chemical disinfectants used in food and industrial areas — Test method and requirements (phase 2, step 1)*

1	2	3	
❑	❑	❑	04/30124414 DC, EN 14185-2, *Non fatty foods — Determination of N-methylcarbamate residues — Part 2: HPLC method with clean-up on a diatomaceous earth column*
❑	❑	❑	99/717087 DC, IEC 61563. Ed.1, *Equipment for measuring specific activity of gamma emitting radionuclides in foodstuffs*
❑	❑	❑	02/712190 DC, ISO 24276, *Foodstuffs — Nucleic acid based methods of analysis for the detection of genetically modified organisms and derived products — General requirements and definitions*
❑	❑	❑	03/303832 DC, EN 14663, *Foodstuffs — Determination of vitamin B6 (including its glycosylated forms) by HPLC*
❑	❑	❑	04/30123521 DC, EN 15054, *Non fatty foods — Determination of chlormequat and mepiquat — LC-MS method*
❑	❑	❑	04/30123525 DC, EN 15055, *Non fatty foods — Determination of chlormequat and mepiquat — LC-MS/MS method*
❑	❑	❑	04/30125026 DC, EN 15086, *Foodstuffs — Determination of isomalt, lactitol, mannitol, sorbitol and xylitol in foodstuffs*
❑	❑	❑	02/123664 DC, BS EN 14538, *Fat and oil derivatives — Fatty acid methyl ester (FAME) — Determination of Ca and Mg content by optical emission spectral analysis with inductively coupled plasma (ICP OES)*

Materials and articles in contact with foodstuffs

1	2	3	
❑	❑	❑	BS EN 631-2:1999, *Materials and articles in contact with foodstuffs — Catering containers — Part 2: Dimensions of accessories and supports*
❑	❑	❑	BS EN 1183:1997, *Materials and articles in contact with foodstuffs — Test methods for thermal shock and thermal shock endurance*
❑	❑	❑	BS EN 1184:1997, *Materials and articles in contact with foodstuffs — Test methods for translucency of ceramic articles*
❑	❑	❑	BS EN 1186-1:2002, *Materials and articles in contact with foodstuffs — Plastics — Part 1: Guide to the selection of conditions and test methods for overall migration*
❑	❑	❑	BS EN 1186-2:2002, *Materials and articles in contact with foodstuffs — Plastics — Part 2: Test methods for overall migration into olive oil by total immersion*
❑	❑	❑	BS EN 1186-3:2002, *Materials and articles in contact with foodstuffs — Plastics — Part 3: Test methods for overall migration into aqueous food simulants by total immersion*
❑	❑	❑	BS EN 1186-4:2002, *Materials and articles in contact with foodstuffs — Plastics — Part 4: Test methods for overall migration into olive oil by cell*
❑	❑	❑	BS EN 1186-5:2002, *Materials and articles in contact with foodstuffs — Plastics — Part 5: Test methods for overall migration into aqueous food simulants by cell*
❑	❑	❑	BS EN 1186-6:2002, *Materials and articles in contact with foodstuffs — Plastics — Part 6: Test methods for overall migration into olive oil using a pouch*
❑	❑	❑	BS EN 1186-7:2002, *Materials and articles in contact with foodstuffs — Plastics — Part 7: Test methods for overall migration into aqueous food simulants using a pouch*
❑	❑	❑	BS EN 1186-8:2002, *Materials and articles in contact with foodstuffs — Plastics — Part 8: Test methods for overall migration into olive oil by article filling*

1	2	3	
❏	❏	❏	BS EN 1186-9:2002, *Materials and articles in contact with foodstuffs — Plastics — Part 9: Test methods for overall migration into aqueous food simulants by article filling*
❏	❏	❏	BS EN 1186-10:2002, *Materials and articles in contact with foodstuffs — Plastics — Part 10: Test methods for overall migration into olive oil (modified method for use in cases where incomplete extraction of olive oil occurs)*
❏	❏	❏	BS EN 1186-11:2002, *Materials and articles in contact with foodstuffs — Plastics — Part 11: Test methods for overall migration into mixtures of C-labelled synthetic triglycerides*
❏	❏	❏	BS EN 1186-12:2002, *Materials and articles in contact with foodstuffs — Plastics — Part 12: Test methods for overall migration at low temperatures*
❏	❏	❏	BS EN 1186-13:2002, *Materials and articles in contact with foodstuffs — Plastics — Part 13: Test methods for overall migration at high temperatures*
❏	❏	❏	BS EN 1186-14:2002, *Materials and articles in contact with foodstuffs — Plastics — Part 14: Test methods for 'substitute tests' for overall migration from plastics intended to come into contact with fatty foodstuffs using test media iso-octane and 95 per cent ethanol*
❏	❏	❏	BS EN 1186-15:2002, *Materials and articles in contact with foodstuffs — Plastics — Part 15: Alternative test methods to migration into fatty food simulants by rapid extraction into iso-octane and/or 95 per cent ethanol*
❏	❏	❏	BS EN 1388-1:1996, *Materials and articles in contact with foodstuffs — Part 1: Silicate surfaces — Determination of the release of lead and cadmium from ceramic ware*
❏	❏	❏	BS EN 1388-2:1996, *Materials and articles in contact with foodstuffs — Part 2: Silicate surfaces — Determination of the release of lead and cadmium from silicate surfaces other than ceramic ware*
❏	❏	❏	BS EN 10333:2005, *Steel for packaging — Flat steel products intended for use in contact with foodstuffs, products or beverages for human and animal consumption — Tin coated steel (tinplate)*
❏	❏	❏	BS EN 10334:2005, *Steel for packaging — Flat steel products intended for use in contact with foodstuffs, products and beverages for human and animal consumption — Non-coated steel (blackplate)*
❏	❏	❏	BS EN 10335:2005, *Steel for packaging — Flat steel products intended for use in contact with foodstuffs, products or beverages for human and animal consumption — Non alloyed electrolytic chromium/chromium oxide coated steel*
❏	❏	❏	BS EN 12546-2:2000, *Materials and articles in contact with foodstuffs — Insulated containers for domestic use — Part 2: Specification for insulated bags and boxes*
❏	❏	❏	BS EN 12546-3:2000, *Materials and articles in contact with foodstuffs — Insulated containers for domestic use — Part 3: Specification for thermal packs*
❏	❏	❏	BS EN 12571:1999, *Materials and articles in contact with foodstuffs — Transport units for catering containers containing prepared foodstuffs — Thermal and hygienic requirements and testing*
❏	❏	❏	BS EN 12855:2003, *Food processing machinery — Rotating bowl cutters — Safety and hygiene requirements*
❏	❏	❏	BS EN 13130-1:2004, *Materials and articles in contact with foodstuffs — Plastics substances subject to limitation — Part 1: Guide to test methods for the specific migration of substances from plastics to foods and food stimulants and the determination of substances in plastics and the selection of conditions of exposure to food stimulants*

1	2	3	
❑	❑	❑	BS EN 13130-2:2004, *Materials and articles in contact with foodstuffs — Plastics substances subject to limitation — Part 2: Determination of terephthalic acid in food simulants*
❑	❑	❑	BS EN 13130-3:2004, *Materials and articles in contact with foodstuffs — Plastics substances subject to limitation — Part 3: Determination of acrylonitrile in food and food simulants*
❑	❑	❑	BS EN 13130-4:2004, *Materials and articles in contact with foodstuffs — Plastics substances subject to limitation — Part 4: Determination of 1,3-butadiene in plastics*
❑	❑	❑	BS EN 13130-5:2004, *Materials and articles in contact with foodstuffs — Plastics substances subject to limitation — Part 5: Determination of vinylidene chloride in food simulants*
❑	❑	❑	BS EN 13130-6:2004, *Materials and articles in contact with foodstuffs — Plastics substances subject to limitation — Part 6: Determination of vinylidene chloride in plastics*
❑	❑	❑	BS EN 13130-7:2004, *Materials and articles in contact with foodstuffs — Plastics substances subject to limitation — Part 7: Determination of monoethylene glycol and diethylene glycol in food simulants*
❑	❑	❑	BS EN 13130-8:2004, *Materials and articles in contact with foodstuffs — Plastics substances subject to limitation — Part 8: Determination of isocyanates in plastics*
❑	❑	❑	DD CEN/TS 13130-9:2005, *Materials and articles in contact with foodstuffs — Plastics substances subject to limitation — Part 9: Determination of acetic acid, vinyl ester in food simulants*
❑	❑	❑	DD CEN/TS 13130-10:2005, *Materials and articles in contact with foodstuffs — Plastics substances subject to limitation — Part 10: Determination of acrylamide in food stimulants*
❑	❑	❑	DD CEN/TS 13130-11:2005, *Materials and articles in contact with foodstuffs — Plastics substances subject to limitation — Part 11: Determination of 11-aminoundecanoic acid in food simulants*
❑	❑	❑	DD CEN/TS 13130-12:2005, *Materials and articles in contact with foodstuffs — Plastics substances subject to limitation — Part 12: Determination of 1,3-benzenedimethaneamine in food simulants*
❑	❑	❑	DD CEN/TS 13130-13:2005, *Materials and articles in contact with foodstuffs — Plastics substances subject to limitation — Part 13: Determination of 2,2-bis(4-hydroxyphenyl)propane (Bisphenol A) in food simulants*
❑	❑	❑	DD CEN/TS 13130-14:2005, *Materials and articles in contact with foodstuffs — Plastics substances subject to limitation — Part 14: Determination of 3,3-bis(3-methyl-4-hydroxyphenyl)2-indolinone in food simulants*
❑	❑	❑	DD CEN/TS 13130-15:2005, *Materials and articles in contact with foodstuffs — Plastics substances subject to limitation — Part 15: Determination of 1,3-butadiene in food simulants*
❑	❑	❑	DD CEN/TS 13130-16:2005, *Materials and articles in contact with foodstuffs — Plastics substances subject to limitation — Part 16: Determination of caprolactam and caprolactam salt in food simulants*
❑	❑	❑	DD CEN/TS 13130-17:2005, *Materials and articles in contact with foodstuffs — Plastics substances subject to limitation — Part 17: Determination of carbonyl chloride in plastics*

1	2	3	
☐	☐	☐	DD CEN/TS 13130-19:2005, *Materials and articles in contact with foodstuffs — Plastics substances subject to limitation — Part 19: Determination of dimethylaminoethanol in food simulants*
☐	☐	☐	DD CEN/TS 13130-20:2005, *Materials and articles in contact with foodstuffs — Plastics substances subject to limitation — Part 20: Determination of epichlorohydrin in plastics*
☐	☐	☐	DD CEN/TS 13130-21:2005, *Materials and articles in contact with foodstuffs — Plastics substances subject to limitation — Part 21: Determination of ethylenediamine and hexamethylenediamine in food simulants*
☐	☐	☐	DD CEN/TS 13130-22:2005, *Materials and articles in contact with foodstuffs — Plastics substances subject to limitation — Part 22: Determination of ethylene oxide and propylene oxide in plastics*
☐	☐	☐	DD CEN/TS 13130-23:2005, *Materials and articles in contact with foodstuffs — Plastics substances subject to limitation — Part 23: Determination of formaldehyde and hexamethylenetetramine in food simulants*
☐	☐	☐	DD CEN/TS 13130-24:2005, *Materials and articles in contact with foodstuffs — Plastics substances subject to limitation — Part 24: Determination of maleic acid and maleic anhydride in food simulants*
☐	☐	☐	DD CEN/TS 13130-25:2005, *Materials and articles in contact with foodstuffs — Plastics substances subject to limitation — Part 25: Determination of 4-methyl-1-pentene in food simulants*
☐	☐	☐	DD CEN/TS 13130-26:2005, *Materials and articles in contact with foodstuffs — Plastics substances subject to limitation — Part 26: Determination of 1-octene and tetrahydrofuran in food simulants*
☐	☐	☐	DD CEN/TS 13130-27:2005, *Materials and articles in contact with foodstuffs — Plastics substances subject to limitation — Part 27: Determination of 2,4,6-triamino-1,3,5-triazine in food simulants*
☐	☐	☐	DD CEN/TS 13130-28:2005, *Materials and articles in contact with foodstuffs — Plastics substances subject to limitation — Part 28: Determination of 1,1,1-trimethylopropane in food simulants*
☐	☐	☐	DD CEN/TS 14234:2002, *Materials and articles in contact with foodstuffs — Polymeric coatings on paper and board — Guide to the selection of conditions and test methods for overall migration*
☐	☐	☐	DD CEN/TS 14235:2002, *Materials and articles in contact with foodstuffs — Polymeric coatings on metal substrates — Guide to the selection of conditions and test methods for overall migration*
☐	☐	☐	BS EN 14338:2003, *Paper and board intended to come into contact with foodstuffs — Conditions for determination of migration from paper and board using modified polyphenylene oxide (MPPO) as a stimulant*
☐	☐	☐	BS EN 601:2004, *Aluminium and aluminium alloys — Castings — Chemical composition of castings for use in contact with foodstuff*
☐	☐	☐	BS EN 602:2004, *Aluminium and aluminium alloys — Wrought products — Chemical composition of semi-finished products used for the fabrication of articles for use in contact with foodstuff*

1	2	3	
❏	❏	❏	BS 6748:1986, *Specification for limits of metal release from ceramic ware, glassware, glass ceramic ware and vitreous enamel ware*
❏	❏	❏	PAS 54:2003, *Specification for domestic ceramicware and glassware — Articles intended for contact with foodstuffs, and vases*
❏	❏	❏	BS EN 1217:1998, *Materials and articles in contact with foodstuffs — Test methods for water absorption of ceramic articles*
❏	❏	❏	BS EN 13258:2003, *Materials and articles in contact with foodstuffs — Test methods for crazing resistance of ceramic articles*
❏	❏	❏	DD CEN/TS 14577:2003, *Materials and articles in contact with foodstuffs — Plastics — Polymeric additives — Test method for the determination of the mass fraction of a polymeric additive that lies below 1 000 Daltons*
❏	❏	❏	BS EN 14233:2002, *Materials and articles in contact with foodstuffs — Plastics — Determination of temperature of plastics materials and articles at the plastics/food interface during microwave and conventional oven heating in order to select the appropriate temperature for migration testing*
❏	❏	❏	BS EN 14481:2003, *Materials and articles in contact with foodstuffs — Plastics — Test methods for the determination of fatty contact*
❏	❏	❏	BS EN 645:1994, *Paper and board intended to come into contact with foodstuffs — Preparation of a cold water extract*
❏	❏	❏	BS EN 646:2001, *Paper and board intended to come into contact with foodstuffs — Determination of colour fastness of dyed paper and board*
❏	❏	❏	BS EN 647:1994, *Paper and board intended to come into contact with foodstuffs — Preparation of a hot water extract*
❏	❏	❏	BS EN 648:2003, *Paper and board intended to come into contact with foodstuffs — Determination of the fastness of fluorescent whitened paper and board*
❏	❏	❏	BS EN 920:2001, *Paper and board intended to come into contact with foodstuffs — Determination of dry matter content in an aqueous extract*
❏	❏	❏	BS EN 1104:2005, *Paper and board intended to come into contact with foodstuffs — Determination of the transfer of antimicrobial constituents*
❏	❏	❏	BS EN 1541:2001, *Paper and board intended to come into contact with foodstuffs — Determination of formaldehyde in an aqueous extract*
❏	❏	❏	BS EN 12497:2005, *Paper and board — Paper and board intended to come into contact with foodstuffs — Determination of mercury in an aqueous extract*
❏	❏	❏	BS EN 12498:2005, *Paper and board — Paper and board intended to come into contact with foodstuffs — Determination of cadmium and lead in an aqueous extract*
❏	❏	❏	BS EN 13676:2001, *Polymer coated paper and board intended for food contact — Detection of pinholes*
❏	❏	❏	BS 7557:1992, *Specification for limits of metal release from painted surfaces of articles, liable to come into contact with foodstuffs*
❏	❏	❏	BS EN 12875-1:2005, *Mechanical dishwashing resistance of utensils — Part 1: Reference test method for domestic articles*
❏	❏	❏	BS EN 12875-2:2002, *Mechanical dishwashing resistance of domestic utensils — Part 2: Inspection of non-metallic articles*

1	2	3	
❏	❏	❏	BS EN ISO 8442-1:1998, *Materials and articles in contact with foodstuffs — Cutlery and table holloware — Part 1: Requirements for cutlery for the preparation of food*
❏	❏	❏	BS EN ISO 8442-2:1998, *Materials and articles in contact with foodstuffs — Cutlery and table holloware — Part 2: Requirements for stainless steel and silver-plated cutlery*
❏	❏	❏	BS EN ISO 8442-3:1998, *Materials and articles in contact with foodstuffs — Cutlery and table holloware — Part 3: Requirements for silver-plated table and decorative holloware*
❏	❏	❏	BS EN ISO 8442-4:1998, *Materials and articles in contact with foodstuffs — Cutlery and table holloware — Part 4: Requirements for gold-plated cutlery*
❏	❏	❏	BS EN ISO 8442-5:2004, *Materials and articles in contact with foodstuffs — Cutlery and holloware — Part 5: Specification for sharpness and edge retention test of cutlery*
❏	❏	❏	BS EN ISO 8442-6:2001, *Materials and articles in contact with foodstuffs — Cutlery and table holloware — Part 6: Lightly silver plated table holloware protected by lacquer*
❏	❏	❏	BS EN ISO 8442-7:2001, *Materials and articles in contact with foodstuffs — Cutlery and table holloware — Part 7: Requirements for table cutlery made of silver, other precious metals and their alloys*
❏	❏	❏	BS EN ISO 8442-8:2001, *Materials and articles in contact with foodstuffs — Cutlery and table holloware — Part 8: Requirements for silver table and decorative holloware*
❏	❏	❏	BS EN 12546-1:2000, *Materials and articles in contact with foodstuffs — Insulated containers for domestic use — Part 1: Specification for vacuum ware, insulated flasks and jugs*
❏	❏	❏	BS EN 12980:2000, *Materials and articles in contact with foodstuffs — Non-metallic articles for catering and industrial use — Method of test for the determination of impact resistance*
❏	❏	❏	BS EN 631-1:1993, *Materials and articles in contact with foodstuffs — Catering containers — Part 1: Specification for dimensions of containers*
❏	❏	❏	05/30136046, DC EN 15284, *Materials and articles in contact with food stuffs — Test method for the resistance of ceramic, glass, glass-ceramic or plastic cookware to microwave heating*
❏	❏	❏	02/703879 DC, prEN 14392, *Aluminium and aluminium alloys — Special requirements for anodised products for use in contact with food*
❏	❏	❏	04/30108996 DC, EN 12875-1, *Mechanical dishwashing resistance of utensils — Part 1: Reference test method for domestic articles*

Plant and equipment for the food industry

1	2	3	
❏	❏	❏	BS 3547:1962, *Specification for electrically-heated food conveyors and carriers*
❏	❏	❏	BS EN 453:2000, *Food processing machinery — Dough mixers — Safety and hygiene requirements*
❏	❏	❏	BS EN 454:2000, *Food processing machinery — Planetary mixers — Safety and hygiene requirements*
❏	❏	❏	BS EN 1672-2:2005, *Food processing machinery — Basic concepts — Part 2: Hygiene requirements*
❏	❏	❏	BS EN 1673:2000, *Food processing machinery — Rotary rack ovens — Safety and hygiene requirements*

1	2	3	
❑	❑	❑	BS EN 1674:2000, *Food processing machinery — Dough and pastry brakes — Safety and hygiene requirements*
❑	❑	❑	BS EN 1678:1998, *Food processing machinery — Vegetable cutting machines — Safety and hygiene requirements*
❑	❑	❑	BS EN 1974:1998, *Food processing machinery — Slicing machines — Safety and hygiene requirements*
❑	❑	❑	BS EN 12041:2000, *Food processing machinery — Moulders — Safety and hygiene requirements*
❑	❑	❑	BS EN 12042:2005, *Food processing machinery — Automatic dividers — Safety and hygiene requirements*
❑	❑	❑	BS EN 12043:2000, *Food processing machinery — Intermediate provers — Safety and hygiene requirements*
❑	❑	❑	BS EN 12267:2003, *Food processing machinery — Circular saw machines — Safety and hygiene requirements*
❑	❑	❑	BS EN 12268:2003, *Food processing machinery — Band saw machines — Safety and hygiene requirements*
❑	❑	❑	BS EN 12355:2003, *Food processing machinery — Derinding-, skinning- and membrane removal machines — Safety and hygiene requirements*
❑	❑	❑	BS EN 12463:2004, *Food processing machinery — Filling machines and auxiliary machines — Safety and hygiene requirements*
❑	❑	❑	BS EN 12505:2000, *Food processing machinery — Centrifugal machines for processing edible oils and fats — Safety and hygiene requirements*
❑	❑	❑	BS EN 12852:2001, *Food processing machinery — Food processors and blenders — Safety and hygiene requirements*
❑	❑	❑	BS EN 12853:2001, *Food processing machinery — Hand-held blenders and whisks — Safety and hygiene requirements*
❑	❑	❑	BS EN 12854:2003, *Food processing machinery — Beam mixers — Safety and hygiene requirements*
❑	❑	❑	BS EN 12984:2005, *Food processing machinery — Portable and/or hand-guided machines and appliances with mechanically driven cutting tools — Safety and hygiene requirements*
❑	❑	❑	BS EN 13208:2003, *Food processing machinery — Vegetable peelers — Safety and hygiene requirements*
❑	❑	❑	BS EN 13288:2005, *Food processing machinery — Bowl lifting and tilting machines — Safety and hygiene requirements.*
❑	❑	❑	BS EN 13289:2001, *Pasta processing plants — Dryers and coolers — Safety and hygiene requirements*
❑	❑	❑	BS EN 13378:2001, *Pasta processing plants — Pasta presses — Safety and hygiene requirements*
❑	❑	❑	BS EN 13379:2001, *Pasta processing plants — Spreader, stripping and cutting machine, stick return conveyor, stick magazine — Safety and hygiene requirements*
❑	❑	❑	BS EN 13389:2005, *Food processing machinery — Mixers with horizontal shafts — Safety and hygiene requirements*

1	2	3	
☐	☐	☐	BS EN 13390:2002, *Food processing machinery — Pie and tart machines — Safety and hygiene requirements*
☐	☐	☐	BS EN 13570:2005, *Food processing machinery — Mixers and mixing machines — Safety and hygiene requirements*
☐	☐	☐	BS EN 13591:2005, *Food processing machinery — Fixed deck oven loaders — Safety and hygiene requirements*
☐	☐	☐	BS EN 13621:2004, *Food processing machinery — Salad dryers — Safety and hygiene requirements*
☐	☐	☐	BS EN 13870:2005, *Food processing machinery — Chop cutting machines — Safety and hygiene requirements*
☐	☐	☐	BS EN 13871:2005, *Food processing machinery — Cubes cutting machinery — Safety and hygiene requirements*
☐	☐	☐	BS EN 13885:2005, *Food processing machinery — Clipping machines — Safety and hygiene requirements*
☐	☐	☐	BS EN 13886:2005, *Food processing machinery — Cooking kettles equipped with powered stirrer and/or mixer — Safety and hygiene requirements*
☐	☐	☐	BS 4825-1:1991, *Stainless steel tubes and fittings for the food industry and other hygienic applications — Part 1: Specification for tubes*
☐	☐	☐	BS 4825-2:1991, *Stainless steel tubes and fittings for the food industry and other hygienic applications — Part 2: Specification for bends and tees*
☐	☐	☐	BS 4825-3:1991, *Stainless steel tubes and fittings for the food industry and other hygienic applications — Part 3: Specification for clamp type couplings*
☐	☐	☐	BS 4825-4:1991, *Stainless steel tubes and fittings for the food industry and other hygienic applications — Part 4: Specification for threaded (IDF type) coupling*
☐	☐	☐	BS 4825-5:1991, *Stainless steel tubes and fittings for the food industry and other hygienic applications — Part 5: Specification for recessed ring joint type couplings*
☐	☐	☐	95/700126 DC, prEN 1672-1, *Food processing machinery — Safety and hygiene requirements — Basic concepts — Part 1: Safety requirements*
☐	☐	☐	96/703609 DC, prEN 12331, *Food processing machinery — Mincing machines — Safety and hygiene requirements*
☐	☐	☐	97/707829 DC, prEN 12851, *Food processing machinery — Catering attachments for machines having an auxiliary drive hub — Safety and hygiene requirements*
☐	☐	☐	99/707700 DC, EN 13534, *Food processing machinery — Curing injection machines — Safety and hygiene requirements*
☐	☐	☐	00/715165 DC, BS EN 13954, *Food processing machinery — Bread slicers — Safety and hygiene requirements*
☐	☐	☐	03/114108 DC, EN 14655, *Food processing machinery — Baguette slicers — Safety and hygiene requirements*

Test methods for a range of products

☐ ☐ ☐ Cereals, Pulses and derived products

☐ ☐ ☐ Fruit and Vegetables

☐ ☐ ☐ Milk and Milk products

☐ ☐ ☐ Meat, Meat products and other Animal products

☐ ☐ ☐ Tea, Coffee and Cocoa

☐ ☐ ☐ Beverages

☐ ☐ ☐ Sugar, Sugar Products and Starch

☐ ☐ ☐ Edible Oils and Fats and Oilseeds

☐ ☐ ☐ Spices, Condiments and Food Additives

Annex 3

Sources of additional information

Good practice

Articles 7–9 of Regulation 852/2004 provide for the development of guides to good practice for hygiene and the application of HACCP principles. Food business operators may use these guides as a voluntary aid to compliance with their obligations under the food hygiene legislation. Further information on good practice guides can be found on the FSA website at:
http://www.food.gov.uk/foodindustry/hygiene/goodpractice

Legislation and regulation

Regulation 1688/2005 was published in the *Official Journal of the European Union (OJ)* of 15 October 2005, L271. Regulations 2073/2005, 2074/2005, 2075/2005 and 2076/2005 were published in the *OJ* of 22 December 2005, L338.

Copies of the Regulations in pdf format can be accessed from the FSA's website at:
http://www.food.gov.uk/foodindustry/regulation/europeleg/eufoodhygieneleg/

Copies of the *OJ* can be accessed from the EU's website at:
http://www.europa.eu.int/eur-lex/lex/JOIndex.do?ihmlang=en

This legislation is applied in the UK by:

– The Food Hygiene (England) Regulations 2006 (SI 2006/14)
– The Food Hygiene (Scotland) Regulations 2006 (SSI 2006/3)
– The Food Hygiene (Wales) Regulations 2006 (SI 2006/31 (W.5))
– The Food Hygiene Regulations (Northern Ireland) 2006 (SR 2006/3)

Copies are obtainable from the Office of Public Sector Information (OPSI).
You can access these from the OPSI website at: http://www.opsi.gov.uk

Background information
Background to the new legislation and copies of the EU texts can be found
on the FSA website at:
http://www.food.gov.uk/foodindustry/regulation/europeleg/eufoodhygieneleg/
     Information for businesses and enforcement practitioners in the form of a
Q&A on the new food hygiene legislation can be accessed from:
http://www.food.gov.uk/foodindustry/hygiene/
     An electronic version of the EU's *OJ* (where the adopted EU regulations
are published) can be found on the EU's website at:
http://www.europa.eu.int/eur-lex/lex/JOIndex.do?ihmlang=en

Meat
http://www.food.gov.uk/foodindustry/meat/
     Includes draft guidance, HACCP diary, wild game and edible co-products.
     On the Microbiological Criteria Regulation:
http://www.food.gov.uk/foodindustry/regulation/europeleg/eufoodhygieneleg/
microbiolreg

Specific to regions

England – 'Safer food, better business'

'Safer food, better business' has been developed by the FSA in partnership with small catering businesses and more than 50 local authorities.

If you would like a 'Safer food, better business' pack then please contact the Environmental Health Department at your local authority or contact FSA Publications on: 0845 606 0667 or email foodstandards@ecgroup.uk.com.

You can also view the pack at:

http://www.food.gov.uk/foodindustry/hygiene/sfbb/

A pack is also being developed for retailers.

Scotland – 'CookSafe'

FSA Scotland has drawn on expertise from the food industry, including small businesses, local authorities and the Scottish Food Advisory Committee to develop an HACCP-based system called 'CookSafe'. Businesses that would like a copy should contact their local authority or this can be downloaded from the FSA website at:

http://www.food.gov.uk/foodindustry/hygiene/cooksafe/

Other sources of information for small businesses from government

The Small Business Service and Business Link

http://www.sbs.gov.uk

http://www.businesslink.gov.uk

Guidance on imports

A document on imports is mainly directed at competent authorities and food businesses in the EU Member States and in third countries with the aim of giving guidance on certain key questions with regard to the implementation of the new food hygiene import requirements and on related subjects. It can be downloaded from the EU website at:

http://www.europa.eu.int/comm/food/international/trade/interpretation_imports.pdf

The Statutory *Food Law Code of Practice* and accompanying *Food Law Practice Guidance* for England and for Wales

This can be found respectively on the FSA's website at:
http://www.food.gov.uk/enforcement/foodlaw/copengland and
http://www.food.gov.uk/multimedia/pdfs/codeofpracticewales.pdf

These were publicized in a letter to enforcers issued via the Enforcement Portal which can be found at:
http://www.food.gov.uk/multimedia/pdfs/enf_e_05_045.pdf.

Hard copies of the above documents can be obtained from the FSA on 020 7276 8455 or 020 7276 8454, or from FSA Wales on 029 2067 8902.

You may also wish to contact environmental/port health representative bodies:

Local Authorities Coordinators of Regulatory Services
http://www.lacors.gov.uk
tel: 020 7840 7200

Chartered Institute of Environmental Health
http://www.cieh.org
tel: 020 7928 6006
email: info@cieh.org

Chartered Institute for Environmental Health Cymru-Wales
http://www.cieh-cymruwales.org
tel: 01766 810081
email: ciehcymruwales@cieh.net

Association of Port Health Authorities
http://www.apha.org.uk
tel: 08707 444505
email: APHA@cieh.org.uk

---

http://www.food.gov.uk/enforcement/
The draft *Code of Practice* and *Practice Guidance for Scotland* can be found on the FSA's website at:
http://www.food.gov.uk/foodindustry/Consultations/consultscot/copscot2005

Hard copies of the above documents can be obtained from Food Standards Agency Scotland on 01224 285118

You may also wish to contact environmental health representative bodies:

Royal Environmental Health Institute of Scotland
www.rehis.org/
tel: 0131 225 6999
email: rehis@rehis.org.uk

Industry organizations and associations
The British Association for Shooting and Conservation
http://www.basc.org.uk

British Egg Industry Service
http://www.britegg.co.uk
tel: 020 7808 9790

British Hospitality Association
http://www.bha-online.org.uk
tel: 0845 880 7744
email: info@bha.org.uk

British Institute of Innkeeping
http://www.bii.org
tel: 01276 684449
email: reception@bii.org

British Meat Processors Association
http://www.bmpa.uk.com
tel: 020 7329 0776
info@bmpa.uk.com

British Poultry Council
http://www.poultry.uk.com
tel: 020 7202 4760
email: white@poultry.uk.com

British Retail Consortium
http://www.brc.org.uk
tel: 020 7854 8900

British Sandwich Association
http://www.sandwich.org.uk
email: admin@sandwich.org.uk

Campden and Chorleywood Food Research Association
http://www.campden.co.uk
tel: 01386 842000

Chilled Food Association
http://www.chilledfood.org
email: cfa@chilledfood.org

Farmers Union of Wales
http://www.fuw.org.uk/

Food and Drink Federation
http://www.fdf.org.uk
tel: 020 7836 2460

Scottish Food and Drink Federation
http://www.sfdf.org.uk
tel: 0131 229 9415

Freight Transport Association
http://www.fta.co.uk
tel: 08717 112222

Hospital Caterers Association
http://www.hospitalcaterers.org
email: alison.mccree@cddah.nhs.uk

Hotel & Catering International Management Association
http://www.hcima.org.uk
tel: 020 8661 4900
email: commdept@hcima.co.uk

Leatherhead Food International
http://www.lfra.co.uk
tel: 01372 376761
email: help@leatherheadfood.com

Meat and Livestock Commission
http://www.mlc.org.uk
tel: 01908 677577

Meat Promotion Wales
http://www.hybucigcymru.org

National Association of Catering Butchers
http://www.nacb.co.uk
tel: 020 7248 1896
email: info@nacb.co.uk

National Farmers' Union
http://www.nfu.org.uk/

National Farmers' Union of Scotland
http://www.nfus.org.uk/

National Farmers' Union (Cymru)
http://www.nfu-cymru.org.uk/

National Pig Association
http://www.npa-uk.net
tel: 020 7331 7650

Nationwide Caterers Association
http://www.ncass.org.uk
tel: 0871 504 1780
email: info@ncass.org.uk

People1st, the Sector Skills Council
http://www.people1st.co.uk
tel: 0870 060 2550

Royal Association of British Dairy Farmers
http://www.rabdf.co.uk
tel: 0845 458 2711
email: office@rabdf.co.uk

Scottish Association of Meat Wholesalers
http://www.scottish-meat-wholesalers.org.uk/

Sea Fish Industry Authority
http://www.seafish.org
tel: 01482 327837

Advice for caterers and consumers is provided on the FSA's websites, http://www.food.gov.uk and http://www.eatwell.gov.uk

If you wish to order any of the publications, please contact FSA Publications:

tel: 0845 606 0667
minicom: 0845 606 0678
fax: 020 8867 3225
email: foodstandards@ecgroup.uk.com

Other general sources of information
To locate your nearest Environmental Health Department please go to: http://www.food.gov.uk/enforcement/yourarea

Annex 4

Index comparing *Managing Food Safety the 22000 Way* against clauses of ISO 22000:2005

ISO 22000 Headings		*Managing Food Safety the 22000 Way*
4.1.	**General Requirements**	**2, 3**
4.2	Documentation requirements	8, 9
4.2.1	General	8, 9
4.2.2	Control of documents	8, 9
4.2.3	Control of records	8, 9
5	**Management responsibility**	
5.1	Management commitment	4, 5, 7, 8, 12
5.2	Food safety policy	4, 5
5.3	Food safety management system planning	5
5.4	Responsibility and authority	5, 8
5.5	Food safety team leader	2, 3, 5

5.6	Communication	8
5.6.1	External communication	8
5.6.2	Internal communication	8
5.7	Emergency preparedness and response	5
5.8	Management review	13
5.8.1	General	13
5.8.2	Review input	5, 13
5.8.3	Review output	13
6	**Resource management**	
6.1.	Provision of resources	8
6.2	Human resources	8
6.2.1	General	8
6.2.2	Competence, awareness and training	8
6.3	Infrastructure	8
6.4	Work environment	8
7	**Planning and realization of safe products**	
7.1	General	5, 6, 8
7.2	PRPs	5, 6, 8
7.3	Preliminary steps to enable hazard analysis	6
7.3.1	General	6
7.3.2	Food safety team	2, 3, 6
7.3.3	Product Characteristics	6
7.3.3.1	Raw materials, ingredients and product-contact materials	6
7.3.3.2	Characteristics of end products	5
7.3.4	Intended use	6

7.3.5	Flow diagrams, process steps and control measures	6
7.3.5.1	Flow diagrams	6
7.3.5.2	Description of process steps and control measures	6
7.4	Hazard analysis	6
7.4.1	General	6
7.4.2	Hazard identification and determination of acceptable levels	6
7.4.3	Hazard assessment	6
7.4.4	Selection and assessment of control measures	6, 8, 10
7.5	Establishing the operational PRPs	6, 8
7.6	Establishing the HACCP plan	6
7.6.1	HACCP plan	6
7.6.2	Identification of CCPs	6
7.6.3	Determination of critical limits for CCPs	6, 10
7.6.4	System for the monitoring of CCPs	6, 10
7.6.5	Actions when monitoring results exceed critical limits	6
7.7	Updating of preliminary information and documents specifying the PRPs and the HACCP plan	10
7.8	Verification planning	10
7.9	Traceability system	6
7.10	Control of nonconformity	5, 10
7.10.1	Corrections	5, 10
7.10.2	Corrective actions	5, 10
7.10.3	Handling of potentially unsafe products	5, 10
7.10.3.1	General	5, 10
7.10.3.2	Evaluation for release	5, 10

7.10.3.3	Disposition of nonconforming products	5, 10
7.10.4	Withdrawals	5, 10
8	**Validation, verification and improvement of the food safety management system**	
8.1	General	10
8.2	Validation of control measure combinations	10
8.3	Control of monitoring and measuring	10
8.4	Food safety management system verification	11
8.4.1	Internal audit	11
8.4.2	Evaluation of individual verification results	11
8.4.3	Analysis of results of verification activities	10, 11
8.5	Improvement	12
8.5.1	Continual improvement	12
8.5.2	Updating the food safety management system	12,13

References

BS EN ISO 9001:2000, *Quality management systems — Requirements*

BS EN ISO 9004:2000, *Quality management systems — Guidelines for performance improvements*

BS EN ISO 14001:2004, *Environmental management systems — Requirements with guidance for use*

BS EN ISO 19011:2002, *Guidelines for quality and/or environmental management systems auditing*

BS EN ISO 22000:2005, *Food safety management systems — Requirements for any organization in the food chain*

ISO/TS 22004:2005, *Food safety management systems — Guidance on the application of ISO 22000:2005*

OHSAS 18001:1999, *Occupational health and safety management systems*

PAS 99:2006, *Specification of common management system requirements as a framework for integration*

Codex Alimentarius. *General principles of food hygiene*. CAC/RCP. 1-1969, REV4. 2003.

BIP 2011, *IMS: Continual improvement through auditing*

BIP 2050, *Managing Safety the Systems Way.*

BIP 2069, *Managing the Environment the 14001 Way.*

BIP 2127, *ISO 22000 Food Safety: Guidance and Workbook for the Catering Industry.*

BIP 2128, *ISO 22000 Food Safety: Guidance and Workbook for the Manufacturing Sector.*

BIP 2129, *ISO 22000 Food Safety: Guidance and Workbook for the Retail Industry.*